Now Serving

THE JUNIOR LEAGUE OF WICHITA FALLS, INC.

United Supermarkets

United Supermarkets, Ltd., is a Texas-based, family-owned retail grocery chain serving twenty-six markets throughout north and west Texas. The company operates forty-six stores under three distinct formats: United Supermarkets, Market Street, and Super Mercado.

Now in its ninety-first year of operation, United traces its roots to 1916, when H. D. Snell opened his first United Cash Store in Sayre, Oklahoma. Through the decades, the company's commitment to its founding values has remained unchanged. The United "spirit" flourishes in the attitudes and enthusiasm of the company's 8,000 team members, who are dedicated to keeping the philosophy alive. From quality product offerings to community involvement, at the heart of United Supermarkets is an unwavering dedication to service. A past winner of the annual Community Service Award from *Supermarket News* and the National Torch Award for Marketplace Ethics from the Council of Better Business Bureaus, United Supermarkets has been named one of the "Best Companies to Work for in Texas" the past two years.

The shared commitment to serving others has resulted in a valued, long-term relationship between United and The Junior League of Wichita Falls. The League's rich history of voluntarism and community enrichment continues to impact the quality of life in our area. United Supermarkets is privileged to continue this partnership by supporting the production and publication of the League's signature cookbook, *Now Serving*.

Now Serving

THE JUNIOR LEAGUE OF WICHITA FALLS, INC.

Now Serving

Published by The Junior League of Wichita Falls, Inc.

Copyright © 2008 by The Junior League of Wichita Falls, Inc.
2302 Midwestern Parkway
Wichita Falls, Texas 76308-2328
940-692-9797

Artwork © by Pamela A. Moller

This cookbook is a collection of favorite recipes,
which are not necessarily original recipes.

Library of Congress Control Number: 2007923583
ISBN: 978-0-9786877-0-0

Edited, Designed, and Manufactured by
Favorite Recipes® Press
An imprint of

FRP®

P. O. Box 305142
Nashville, Tennessee 37230
800-358-0560

Art Director and Book Design: Steve Newman
Project Editor: Linda A. Jones

Manufactured in China
First Printing: 2008
10,000 copies

Acknowledgments

The Junior League of Wichita Falls, Inc. extends special thanks to those who generously assisted with the production of *Now Serving*.

Pamela A. Moller, artist, is a Wichita Falls, Texas native. She is a graduate of Notre Dame Catholic School and received a Bachelor of Fine Arts degree from Midwestern State University in 1981. Moller is a well-known regional artist whose unique works are highly regarded within the local community. In addition to creating and selling ceramics, she also has designed many commercial and residential interiors and frequently shares her time and talents with community organizations. Ms. Moller is married to Larry Simpson and has two sons.

Gary Goldberg, graphic artist, is a professor of art at Midwestern State University in Wichita Falls, Texas. His work has been published in several books and magazines, including *Texas Monthly*. Professor Goldberg has been awarded a grant from the National Endowment for the Arts, and his work appears in many collections, including the Library of Congress, the Harry Ransom Humanities Research Center, and the University of Texas at Austin.

KFDX 3/Texoma's FOX, Media Partner

United Supermarkets/Market Street, Community Partner

The Junior League of Wichita Falls, Inc. Cookbook Committee

CHAIRMEN
Leslie Hawthorne and Paula Perkins

CHAIRMEN-ELECT
Lindsay Greer and Paula Perkins

COMMITTEE MEMBERS
Shawn Butler
  Secretary/Treasurer
Lindsay Greer
  Writing/Editing and Marketing
Jennifer McDonald
  Art/Design
Traci Neiman
  Recipes

SUSTAINING ADVISORS
Claudette Burlison
Sue Crosnoe
Dee Ann Martin
Gale Richardson
Debbie White
Pat Wolverton

PRESIDENT, 2005–2006
Leah Ford

PRESIDENT, 2006–2007
Denise Moffat

PRESIDENT, 2007–2008
Katie Parkey

Table of Contents

Appetizers & Beverages

Breads & Breakfast

Soups & Salads

Main Dishes

Introduction

The Junior League of Wichita Falls, Inc. is proud to present *Now Serving*, the newest addition to our history of cookbooks. Since the League's first cookbook, *Discoveries in Dining* in 1960, followed by *Home Cookin'* in 1976, times have certainly changed. More League volunteers work outside the home than ever before and therefore need simple yet tasty meals to serve their families.

Even though we may not spend all day in the kitchen anymore, we still have the same purpose as our predecessors. *Now Serving* is a tribute to that purpose— to not only serve our families a wonderful meal, but also to serve our community through many volunteer hours and projects.

Now Serving is a compilation of new and perhaps easier recipes, but it is also peppered with classics from our earlier cookbooks. In this book, you will find regional favorites, a little comfort food, and great entertaining recipes, along with helpful tips to make your time in the kitchen more efficient.

The contents of this book are the mealtime experiences of not only the families of our members, but also our members' friends. To both we are truly grateful. The recipes are not all originals, but they do represent family favorites. We hope you enjoy *Now Serving* and that it becomes a staple in your kitchen, one you turn to time and time again. Just as our previous cookbooks have been passed along through the generations, *Now Serving* is one that will be treasured for years to come.

History

The Junior League of Wichita Falls, Inc.

In 1957, twenty-two women with social consciences saw the need for a woman's service organization. The result of their vision was the Junior Service League of Wichita Falls. These women quickly went to work, participating in the formation of the Arts Council and the Junior Red Cross. Those efforts were soon followed with training the first case investigators for the City-County Welfare Department and a partnership with other organizations to provide hearing tests for local schoolchildren.

Junior Service League members embraced their biggest challenge to date in 1964. Along with voting to make a formal application to the Association of Junior Leagues for full membership, the members finalized plans for the Wichita Falls Museum and Art Center.

Two years later, the Junior Service League initiated a partnership with the German squadron of the Euro-NATO Joint Jet Pilot Training program (ENJJPT) at Sheppard Air Force Base that endures today. As the longest running project of the Junior League, the International Friendship Committee continues to host functions and attend activities with the German squadron to promote lasting friendships and to welcome these visitors into our country and our community.

In 1969 the Junior Service League officially became The Junior League of Wichita Falls, Inc., making it one of 211 Junior Leagues active at the time.

Throughout the 1970s, Junior League volunteers championed drug education programs in the local elementary schools. Furthermore, the League voted to work toward opening a facility for the blind, and on June 6, 1974, Beacon Lights became incorporated. The Junior League also worked with organizers to start a child advocacy program, later known as Child Advocates, or CASA. In addition, Goodtime Singers, a group that provides music therapy to nursing home residents within the community, was formed in 1975. Still touring their music and good cheer today, the group serenades residents with old classics, favorite hymns, and native Texas songs accompanied by tambourines, a cowbell, a train whistle, a washboard, and a gut bucket.

During the 1980s, The Junior League of Wichita Falls, Inc. partnered with the Wichita Falls Police Department to develop the Crime Stoppers program. Then in 1981 a Junior League tradition began with the first Christmas Magic, now a three-day shopping festival with over 125 merchants and 10,000 shoppers. Over the past twenty-five years, this holiday event has funded hundreds of thousands of dollars in projects and community services.

In 1986 the Junior League partnered with the City of Wichita Falls and Streams and Valleys, Inc. to organize FallsFest. What started out as a project for the community is now the largest outdoor festival in the region. Proceeds from this event have helped fund such community initiatives as River Bend Nature Center, the Wee-Chi-Tah sculpture, Berend's Landing, and parks and green space development within the city.

The membership focus shifted toward children's health in the early 1990s. During that time, 230 Leagues nationwide, including Wichita Falls, participated in a public awareness campaign to encourage early childhood immunizations. Environmental issues were also a topic of interest among League members, and in 1991, The Junior League of Wichita Falls, Inc. adopted the environment as a Focus Area. Work began on a collaborative arrangement with the City of Wichita Falls to develop a regional environmental center. Ground was broken for River Bend Nature Works in 1995, which is now its own independent nonprofit organization. The 1990s also saw the successful launch of Teen Court in 1997. This collaboration with the Boys and Girls Club of Wichita Falls offers misdemeanor teen offenders alternatives to the judicial system.

A new century brought new opportunity to The Junior League of Wichita Falls, Inc. To celebrate the centennial of the Association of Junior Leagues International, the League spearheaded the realization of a dream of the local Habitat for Humanity organization. In 2001–2002, the League coordinated and partially funded Wichita Falls' first "All Women Build" for Habitat for Humanity.

During 2004–2005, the Research and Development committee of The Junior League of Wichita Falls, Inc. actively pursued many options for a signature project to bring to the community. After a year of research, the membership voted to build a Miracle League Field of Dreams, a specially designed, adaptive baseball field with total accessibility for children with disabilities and special needs.

Today, thousands of volunteer hours and millions of dollars later, The Junior League of Wichita Falls, Inc. continues to fulfill the vision of the Junior Service League members. We remain a diverse and dynamic group of talented women who share a common desire to improve the quality of life in Wichita Falls. With over 380 active, provisional, and sustaining members, this organization contributes over 17,000 volunteer hours and over $300,000 annually in training and project funding to the Wichita Falls community. For fifty years, The Junior League of Wichita Falls, Inc. has been instrumental in improving the community through the leadership and commitment of trained volunteers. And, we look forward with anticipation to the next generation of Junior League volunteers.

Many thanks to Leslie Schaffner, sustaining member, who graciously provided
***A Century of Progress**, a comprehensive written article that served as foundational
information appearing in the **History of The Junior League of Wichita Falls, Inc.***

Our Mission

The Junior League of Wichita Falls, Inc. is an organization
of women committed to promoting voluntarism, developing
the potential of women, and improving our community
through the effective action and leadership of trained volunteers.
Our purpose is exclusively educational and charitable.

Appetizers & Beverages

*"Food . . . can look beautiful, taste exquisite, smell wonderful,
make people feel good, bring them together, inspire romantic feelings.
At its most basic, it is fuel for a hungry machine."*

—Rosamond Richardson

*"Happy and successful cooking doesn't rely on know-how;
it comes from the heart, makes great demands on the palate, and needs
enthusiasm and a deep love of food to bring it to life."*

—Georges Blanc

"Make food simple and let things taste of what they are."

—Maurice Edmond Sailland

Pamela A Möller
2007 ©

Brie and Mango Quesadillas

1/2 cup water
1/2 yellow onion, thinly sliced and
  cut into halves
2 poblano chiles, roasted,
  peeled and chopped
1 mango, chopped

4 1/2 tablespoons butter, melted
1/4 cup vegetable oil
10 flour tortillas
1 pound Brie cheese or
  Camembert cheese,
  cut into 1/4-inch strips

Heat the water in a medium skillet over high heat. Add the onion and remove from the heat. Let stand for 12 minutes or until the onion slices are tender; drain. Mix the poblano chiles and mango in a small bowl. Blend the butter and oil in a small bowl.

Heat a nonstick or well-seasoned skillet over medium heat for several minutes. Place one tortilla in the hot skillet and heat for 15 seconds on each side until softened. Place a few strips of the Brie cheese on half of the tortilla. Add several onion strips and 1 tablespoon of the mango mixture. Fold the other half of the tortilla over the filling and brush with the melted butter mixture. Repeat with the remaining tortillas.

Brown the quesadillas one at a time on both sides in a hot skillet over medium heat. Place on a baking sheet and keep warm in a 200-degree oven. Cut each quesadilla into three triangular wedges to serve.

Makes 30 wedges

Honey Walnut-Encrusted
Pear Crostini

1 large ripe pear, peeled, cored
  and chopped
2 tablespoons sugar
24 (1/2-inch) slices Italian or
  French bread

1/4 cup olive oil
4 ounces blue cheese, crumbled
1/3 cup chopped walnuts
2 tablespoons honey

Combine the pear and sugar in a bowl and toss to coat. Place the bread on a baking sheet. Brush each slice with the olive oil. Broil for 45 seconds. Top each with the pear mixture, blue cheese and walnuts. Return to the oven and broil for 45 seconds longer or until the blue cheese melts. Remove from the oven and arrange the crostini on a platter for presentation. Drizzle with the honey before serving.

Makes 2 dozen

Artichoke Bruschetta

1 French baguette
1 (6-ounce) jar marinated
    artichoke hearts, drained
    and chopped

^{1}/$_2$ to ^{3}/$_4$ cup (2 to 3 ounces)
    grated Romano cheese
^{1}/$_3$ cup finely chopped red onion
5 tablespoons mayonnaise

Cut the baguette into slices ^{1}/$_3$ inch thick. Mix the artichoke hearts, Romano cheese, onion and mayonnaise in a bowl. Spread equal amounts of the artichoke mixture over the baguette slices. Arrange the slices in a single layer on a large baking sheet. Broil for 2 minutes or until light brown and bubbly.

Serves 8

Asparagus Mushroom Tostados

4 fresh asparagus spears
2 tablespoons chopped onion
2 tablespoons olive oil
1 garlic clove, finely chopped
2 cups sliced shiitake mushrooms
2 tablespoons white wine

1 teaspoon chopped fresh basil
1 teaspoon chopped fresh marjoram
1 teaspoon chopped fresh thyme
16 round tortilla chips
6 ounces smoked Gruyère cheese,
    cut into 16 pieces

Snap off the tough ends of the asparagus spears. Cook the asparagus spears in boiling water in a saucepan for 3 minutes or until tender-crisp. Plunge into ice water to stop the cooking process. Drain and cut into ^{1}/$_2$-inch pieces.

Sauté the onion in hot olive oil in a large skillet over medium heat for 30 seconds or until tender. Add the garlic and mushrooms and sauté for 1 to 2 minutes or until the mushrooms are tender. Add the wine and cook for 2 minutes, stirring to loosen the brown bits from the bottom of the skillet. Stir in the basil, marjoram, thyme and asparagus.

Place the tortilla chips in a single layer on a baking sheet. Spoon 1 teaspoon of the mushroom mixture onto each tortilla chip and top evenly with the Gruyère cheese. Bake at 350 degrees for 5 to 10 minutes or until the cheese melts.

Serves 8

Avocado Wraps

DIPPING SAUCE
1/2 cup cashews, chopped
2/3 cup fresh cilantro, chopped
2 garlic cloves, quartered
2 green onions, chopped
1 tablespoon sugar
1 teaspoon freshly ground pepper
1 teaspoon cumin
4 teaspoons white vinegar
1 teaspoon balsamic vinegar
1/2 teaspoon tamarind pulp
1/2 cup honey
Pinch of powdered saffron
1/4 cup olive oil

WRAPS
1 large avocado, peeled, pitted
   and chopped
2 tablespoons chopped sun-dried
   tomatoes packed in oil
1 tablespoon minced red onion
1/2 teaspoon chopped fresh cilantro
Pinch of salt
Dash of lime juice
3 egg roll wraps
1 egg, beaten
1 cup vegetable oil for frying

To prepare the sauce, pulse the cashews, cilantro, garlic, green onions, sugar, pepper and cumin in a food processor until blended. Combine the white vinegar, balsamic vinegar, tamarind pulp, honey and saffron in a small microwave-safe bowl. Microwave on High for 1 minute. Stir until the tamarind is dissolved. Add to the cashew mixture and pulse with short bursts for 20 seconds or until combined. Pour into a small bowl. Stir in the olive oil. Cover and chill for at least 1 hour before serving.

To prepare the wraps, place the avocado, sun-dried tomatoes, onion, cilantro, salt and lime juice in a small bowl and stir gently to mix. Lay the egg roll wraps on a clean surface with the points forming a diamond shape. Place one-third of the avocado mixture in the middle of each wrap and spread to within 1 inch of each edge. Fold the bottom point of the wrap over the top of the filling, brushing the remaining corners and edges of the wrapper with the beaten egg. Fold the sides in toward the middle. Finish by rolling up over the top point of the wrapper to seal and prevent leakage. Repeat with the remaining wraps. Chill in the refrigerator until ready to deep-fry.

Deep-fry the wraps in 375-degree oil in a deep fryer or deep pan for 3 to 4 minutes or until golden brown. Remove to paper towels to drain and cool. Slice the wraps diagonally across the middle and arrange on a serving plate around a small bowl of the dipping sauce.

Makes 3 wraps

Stuffed Mushrooms

24 fresh mushrooms, 1 1/2 to
   2 inches in diameter, rinsed
   and drained
1/4 cup sliced green onions
1 garlic clove, minced

1/4 cup (1/2 stick) butter
2/3 cup fine dry bread crumbs
1/2 cup (2 ounces) shredded
   Cheddar cheese or crumbled
   blue cheese

Remove the mushroom stems, reserving the caps. Chop enough of the mushroom stems to measure 1 cup. Cook the chopped mushroom stems, green onions and garlic in the butter in a medium saucepan until tender. Stir in the bread crumbs and Cheddar cheese. Spoon into the reserved mushroom caps. Arrange the mushrooms in a 10×15-inch baking pan. Bake at 425 degrees for 8 to 10 minutes or until heated through.

Serves 12

Mushroom Toastwists

1 cup cream of mushroom soup
1/2 cup black olives, chopped
2 green onions, finely chopped

1/8 teaspoon Worcestershire sauce
2 loaves of bread
1/2 cup (1 stick) butter, melted

Combine the soup, black olives, green onions and Worcestershire sauce in a bowl and mix well. Trim the crusts from the bread. Roll each slice of bread thin with a rolling pin. Place 1 teaspoon of the soup mixture on each slice of bread and roll up tightly to enclose the filling. Dip in the butter and place on a baking sheet lined with waxed paper. Freeze until firm.

To serve, place the roll-ups on a baking sheet and bake at 350 degrees for 10 minutes or until crisp and golden brown.

Makes 4 dozen

Polenta Squares with Mushroom Ragù

POLENTA

2 cups water

1 tablespoon butter, softened

1/2 teaspoon salt, or to taste

1/2 cup quick-cooking polenta

MUSHROOM RAGÙ

1 tablespoon olive oil

8 ounces cremini mushrooms,
    chopped

1/2 cup chopped onion

1/2 teaspoon salt, or to taste

1/4 teaspoon freshly ground
    pepper, or to taste

1 garlic clove, minced

3/4 cup dry marsala

1/2 teaspoon all-purpose flour

2 tablespoons butter, softened

2 tablespoons chopped fresh
    Italian parsley leaves

To prepare the polenta, bring the water, butter and salt to a boil in a heavy medium saucepan. Whisk in the polenta gradually. Reduce the heat to medium-low. Cook for 5 minutes or until thickened, stirring constantly. Pour into a greased 9×9-inch baking pan, spreading about 1/3 inch thick. Cover and let stand at room temperature for 15 minutes or until set.

To prepare the mushroom ragù, heat the olive oil in a heavy large skillet over medium-high heat. Add the mushrooms and onion. Season with the salt and pepper. Sauté for 8 minutes or until the juices evaporate. Add the garlic and sauté for 2 minutes or until the mushrooms are golden brown. Reduce the heat to medium-low. Add the marsala. Cover and simmer for 5 minutes or until the marsala is reduced by one-half. Mix the flour and butter in a small bowl to form a paste. Stir the paste into the mushroom mixture. Cover and simmer for 2 minutes or until the sauce thickens slightly. Remove from the heat and stir in the parsley.

To serve, cut the polenta into thirty-six bite-size squares and spoon the warm ragù on top.

Makes 3 dozen

FRESH SALSA

Try serving Fresh Salsa atop the polenta squares. To prepare, chop 1/4 medium onion and 4 green onions. Mix with one 28-ounce can diced tomatoes, one 4-ounce can chopped green chiles, 1 tablespoon chopped jalapeño chiles, 1 tablespoon cider vinegar, 1 1/2 teaspoons cumin, 1/4 teaspoon minced garlic, chopped cilantro, salt and pepper to taste in a bowl. Let stand for the flavors to blend before serving. Makes 4 cups.

Tomato Cheese Pie

1 pound Gruyère cheese, cut into
    paper-thin slices
3 or 4 tomatoes, peeled, sliced
    and drained
1 partially baked (9-inch) pie shell
1 teaspoon basil

1 to 2 teaspoons dill weed
Salt and freshly ground pepper
    to taste
2 tablespoons grated Parmesan cheese
2 tablespoons butter, softened
    or melted

Place a layer of the Gruyère cheese and tomatoes in the partially baked pie shell.
Season with some of the basil, dill weed, salt and pepper. Sprinkle with some
of the Parmesan cheese and dot with some of the butter. Repeat the layers until
all the ingredients are used. Bake at 375 degrees for 20 to 25 minutes or until
the cheese melts.

Serves 8

Bacon Cheese Bites

3 cups (12 ounces) shredded sharp
    Cheddar cheese
1 (4-ounce) can sliced black olives
1 cup finely sliced green onions
1/4 to 1/2 cup chopped green chiles

1 cup mayonnaise
1 cup crumbled crisp bacon
1 (16-ounce) package cocktail
    rye bread

Combine the Cheddar cheese, olives, green onions, green chiles, mayonnaise
and bacon in a bowl and mix well. Spread on each slice of the bread and place
on a baking sheet. Bake at 300 degrees for 15 to 20 minutes or until bubbly.
(Note: You may prepare ahead and freeze before baking.)

Serves 8

Water Chestnuts Take a Wrap

24 canned whole water
chestnuts, drained
4 teaspoons soy sauce

1 tablespoon sherry
12 slices lean bacon
4 to 6 tablespoons brown sugar

Combine the water chestnuts, soy sauce and sherry in a bowl and toss to coat. Marinate, covered, in the refrigerator for 2 to 4 hours. (Marinating the water chestnuts longer will result in a crunchier texture and an enhanced flavor.)

Cut each bacon strip into halves and place in rows on a tray. Sprinkle with the brown sugar. Drain the water chestnuts, discarding the marinade. Place one water chestnut at the end of each bacon half and roll up, securing with wooden picks. Place the roll-ups on a baking sheet lined with foil. Bake at 425 degrees on the upper oven rack for 15 to 20 minutes or until the bacon is cooked through. (Note: To bake ahead, bake the roll-ups for 10 minutes and chill in the refrigerator. To serve, bake for 5 to 7 minutes or until the bacon is cooked through. You may cut the water chestnuts into halves if too large.)

Makes 2 dozen

Grilled Stuffed Jalapeños

8 ounces chicken tenders
3/4 cup Italian salad dressing
4 ounces cream cheese, softened
1/8 teaspoon salt

1/8 teaspoon pepper
12 jalapeño chiles, about 31/2 to
4 inches long
12 thin slices bacon

Place the chicken and 1/2 cup of the salad dressing in a shallow dish or a sealable plastic bag. Cover the dish or seal the bag and marinate in the refrigerator for 30 minutes. Drain the chicken, discarding the marinade. Place the chicken on a grill rack and grill, covered, over medium heat for 4 to 5 minutes on each side or until the chicken is cooked through, basting with the remaining 1/4 cup salad dressing. Cool the chicken slightly and finely chop.

Mix the chicken, cream cheese, salt and pepper in a bowl. (You may also process in a food processor.) Cut the jalapeño chiles lengthwise down one side and remove the seeds. Spoon 11/2 to 2 tablespoons of the chicken mixture into each jalapeño chile. Wrap each jalapeño chile with one slice of the bacon and secure with wooden picks. Place on a grill rack. Grill over medium heat for 20 to 25 minutes or until the bacon is crisp and cooked through, turning frequently.

Makes 2 dozen

Shrimp Artichoke Marinée

1 egg yolk
1/4 cup red wine vinegar
3/4 cup vegetable oil
2 tablespoons (or less) dry mustard
2 tablespoons chopped parsley
2 tablespoons chopped scallions
2 tablespoons chopped chives

1 pound number 2 shrimp, cooked
2 (6-ounce) cans artichoke
    hearts, drained
1 cup chili sauce
1 garlic clove, minced
2 tablespoons drained horseradish
2 tablespoons chopped parsley

Blend the egg yolk, wine vinegar, oil, dry mustard, 2 tablespoons parsley, the scallions and chives in a bowl. Stir in the shrimp and artichoke hearts. Marinate, covered, in the refrigerator for 24 hours. Mix the chili sauce, garlic, horseradish and 2 tablespoons parsley in a bowl. Drain the shrimp mixture and serve on crackers topped with the sauce. (Note: If you are concerned about using raw egg yolks, use yolks from eggs pasteurized in their shells, which are sold at some specialty food stores, or use an equivalent amount of pasteurized egg substitute.)

Serves 8

Crabbies

1/2 cup (1 stick) butter, softened
1 cup (4 ounces) shredded
    mozzarella cheese
1 cup soft pimento cheese spread
2 tablespoons mayonnaise
1 garlic clove, minced
2 or 3 dashes of Tabasco sauce

8 ounces crab meat, shells removed
    and flaked
8 English muffins, split
Salt to taste
1 cup (4 ounces) shredded
    Cheddar cheese

Mix the butter, mozzarella cheese and pimento cheese spread in a bowl. Stir in the mayonnaise, garlic, Tabasco sauce and crab meat. Spread on the muffin halves and season with salt. Sprinkle with the Cheddar cheese. Place on a baking sheet and broil until golden brown. Cut each muffin half into six wedges and serve.

Makes 8 dozen

PIMENTO CHEESE SPREAD

Combine 3 cups (12 ounces) shredded sharp Cheddar cheese, 8 ounces chive and onion cream cheese, softened, a drained 4-ounce jar of pimentos and 1/2 cup chopped toasted pecans in a bowl and mix well. Chill in the refrigerator. Makes 2 1/2 cups.

Smoked Salmon and Herbed Cheese Roulade

12 cups spinach	8 ounces cream cheese, softened
3 egg yolks	2 tablespoons finely chopped fresh
1 teaspoon salt	dill weed
1/2 teaspoon pepper	Grated zest and juice of 1 lemon
1/4 teaspoon ground nutmeg	Salt and pepper to taste
3 egg whites	8 ounces smoked salmon slices

Cook the spinach in boiling water in a saucepan until wilted. Drain and blanch in cold water. Squeeze the spinach dry. Process the spinach, egg yolks, 1 teaspoon salt, 1/2 teaspoon pepper and nutmeg in a food processor or blender until puréed. Beat the egg whites at high speed in a mixing bowl until soft peaks form. Fold gently into the spinach mixture. Spread in a 10×15-inch baking pan lined with buttered baking parchment. Bake at 400 degrees for 10 to 12 minutes or until set. Invert the roulade onto baking parchment and let stand until cool. Beat the cream cheese, dill weed, lemon zest, lemon juice, salt and pepper to taste in a bowl until smooth. Peel off the baking parchment from the roulade and cut the roulade into halves crosswise. Place each half on a sheet of plastic wrap. Spread the cream cheese mixture evenly over each half to 1/2 inch from the edges. Cover each with a layer of the salmon and sprinkle with pepper to taste. Roll up each half from the long edge and wrap in plastic wrap, twisting the ends. Chill for 1 hour. Remove the plastic wrap and trim the ends of each roulade with a serrated knife. Cut each roulade into ten pieces. Serve chilled or at room temperature. (Note: The roulades can be made one day ahead.)

Makes 20 pieces

Shrimp Dip Magnifico

12 ounces cream cheese, softened	2 pounds large shrimp, cooked,
1 cup Thousand Island	peeled, deveined and chopped
salad dressing	4 teaspoons Tabasco sauce
1/2 cup mayonnaise	1 tablespoon seasoned salt
1 cup minced green onions	1 tablespoon prepared horseradish

Beat the cream cheese, salad dressing and mayonnaise in a mixing bowl until blended. Stir in the green onions, shrimp, Tabasco sauce, seasoned salt and horseradish. Chill, covered, for 6 to 8 hours. Serve with assorted party crackers.

Serves 8 to 10

Creamy Caviar

8 ounces cream cheese, softened
8 ounces cottage cheese, drained
2 tablespoons whipping cream
3/4 teaspoon grated onion

1 teaspoon lemon juice
Thin lemon slices
Caviar

Press the cream cheese and cottage cheese through a sieve into a mixing bowl. Beat in the whipping cream gradually. Add the onion and lemon juice and beat until mixed. Prepare a coeur à la crème mold or perforated mold and fill with the cheese mixture. Chill for 8 to 10 hours. Unmold onto a serving platter. Surround with thin lemon slices and caviar. Serve with wafer crackers.

Serves 24

Artichoke Crab Dip

3 (6-ounce) jars marinated
    artichoke hearts, drained
2 (6-ounce) cans crab meat, chopped
16 ounces Parmesan
    cheese, shredded

1 1/2 cups mayonnaise
4 ounces cream cheese, softened
1 teaspoon lemon juice
Salt to taste
Dash of red pepper

Mix the artichoke hearts, crab meat, Parmesan cheese, mayonnaise, cream cheese, lemon juice, salt and red pepper in a microwave-safe bowl. Microwave on High for 5 minutes. Remove from the microwave and stir. Microwave on High for 5 minutes longer. Serve with pita crisps or garlic melba toast. (Note: You may use 1 package imitation crab meat.)

Serves 12 to 15

Hot Bacon Heart Attack

8 ounces cream cheese, softened
1/2 cup mayonnaise
1 cup (4 ounces) shredded Swiss cheese
2 tablespoons chopped green onions
8 slices bacon, cooked and crumbled
1/2 cup crushed butter crackers

Combine the cream cheese, mayonnaise, Swiss cheese and green onions in a bowl and mix well. Spoon into a baking dish. Sprinkle with the bacon and crushed crackers. Bake at 350 degrees for 20 minutes. Serve with butter crackers or other assorted crackers.

Serves 6

Islander Cheese Ball

16 ounces cream cheese, softened
1 (8-ounce) can crushed pineapple, drained
1/4 cup chopped bell pepper
2 tablespoons chopped green onions
2 teaspoons seasoned salt
2 cups chopped pecans

Beat the cream cheese and pineapple in a mixing bowl until smooth. Stir in the bell pepper, green onions, seasoned salt and 1/2 cup of the pecans. Shape into a ball or spoon into a pineapple boat. Roll in or top with the remaining pecans. Serve with bacon-flavored crackers.

Serves 4 to 6

South-of-the-Border Guacamole

1/2 cup chopped white onion
2 or 3 serrano chiles,
   seeded and chopped
1/4 cup cilantro, chopped
3 or 4 garlic cloves, finely chopped
1 teaspoon salt
1/8 teaspoon black pepper

3 or 4 ripe avocados
1 tablespoon fresh lime juice
1 tablespoon fresh lemon juice
3/4 cup drained chopped seeded
   Roma tomatoes
Pinch of cayenne pepper

Process the onion, serrano chiles, cilantro, garlic, salt and black pepper in a food processor until blended. Pit and dice the avocados. Coarsely mash the avocados in a bowl. Stir in the lime juice and lemon juice. Fold in the onion mixture. Stir in the tomatoes. Sprinkle with the cayenne pepper and serve immediately. (Note: If a spicier guacamole is desired, add serrano chile seeds to taste. Use 1 garlic clove for each avocado used.)

Serves 12

Chutney Cheese Spread

8 ounces cream cheese with
   chives, softened
8 ounces sharp Cheddar cheese,
   shredded

2 tablespoons dry sherry
1 teaspoon curry powder
1/8 teaspoon Tabasco sauce
Favorite chutney or relish

Process the cream cheese, Cheddar cheese, sherry, curry powder and Tabasco sauce in a food processor until smooth. Line a pie plate or bowl with waxed paper. Spoon the cheese mixture into the prepared pie plate or bowl. Chill or freeze until set. Invert onto a serving platter. Spoon the chutney over the top and serve with assorted crackers.

Serves 8

CRANBERRY RELISH

Process one 16-ounce package fresh cranberries, 1 navel orange and 1 apple separately in a food processor until grated. Combine the cranberries, orange, apple, 1 3/4 cups sugar and one 3-ounce package raspberry gelatin in a large bowl and mix well. Stir in 1 cup finely chopped pecans. Chill, covered, in the refrigerator. Serves 12.

Spinach Dip

1 onion, finely chopped
2 tablespoons butter
3 Roma tomatoes, finely chopped
1 (4-ounce) can chopped green
    chiles, drained
2 (15-ounce) cans spinach, drained

8 ounces cream cheese, softened
1 cup half-and-half
2 cups (8 ounces) shredded
    Monterey Jack cheese
Salt and pepper to taste
2 tablespoons sour cream

Sauté the onion in the butter in a skillet until tender. Add the tomatoes and green chiles and cook for 2 minutes. Spoon into a large bowl. Add the spinach, cream cheese, half-and-half and Monterey Jack cheese and mix well. Season with salt and pepper. Spoon into a shallow baking dish and bake at 400 degrees for 35 minutes or until the dip is bubbly and the top is light brown. Top with the sour cream before serving.

Serves 8

Hummus Dip

2 (16-ounce) cans chick-peas,
    rinsed and drained
3 garlic cloves
1/2 cup drained roasted red
    bell peppers
1/2 cup tahini
1/4 cup water

2 tablespoons olive oil
1/2 teaspoon cumin
1/4 teaspoon red pepper,
    or to taste
1 1/2 teaspoons salt
1/3 to 1/2 cup lime juice
Flat-leaf parsley

Process the chick-peas, garlic, bell peppers, tahini, water, olive oil, cumin, red pepper and salt in a food processor until combined. Add the lime juice gradually, processing constantly until smooth. Spoon into a serving bowl and garnish with flat-leaf parsley.

Serves 6 to 8

TOASTED SESAME PITA BREAD

Split 6 pita bread rounds into halves horizontally. Cut each half into eight triangles and arrange in a single layer on a baking sheet. Brush with 6 tablespoons melted butter or olive oil. Sprinkle with about 2 tablespoons sesame seeds, minced garlic to taste, 1/4 teaspoon salt and 1/2 teaspoon pepper. Bake at 375 degrees for 10 to 13 minutes or until toasted. A perfect accompaniment with Hummus Dip. Makes 8 dozen.

Tzatziki

16 ounces plain yogurt
2 cucumbers, peeled, seeded and
   finely chopped
1 1/2 tablespoons olive oil
1 tablespoon chopped fresh
   dill weed

3 garlic cloves, minced
1 teaspoon red wine vinegar
1 teaspoon salt
1/4 teaspoon pepper
Dash of lemon juice
Thinly sliced cucumbers

Spoon the yogurt into a coffee filter suspended over a bowl. Let stand in the refrigerator for 2 hours to drain. Wrap the finely chopped cucumbers in a paper towel and squeeze to remove the liquid. Combine the drained yogurt, drained cucumber, olive oil, dill weed, garlic, wine vinegar, salt, pepper and lemon juice in a medium bowl and stir to mix. Spoon into a serving dish. Chill, covered, for at least 2 hours. Garnish with thinly sliced cucumbers before serving. Serve atop pita bread with melted feta cheese or as a sauce for other Greek dishes.

Serves 4

Texas Caviar

1 (16-ounce) jar salsa
2 (16-ounce) cans black-eyed
   peas, drained
1 (16-ounce) can white
   hominy, drained
1 cup chopped green bell pepper
1 cup chopped white onion
1 cup chopped tomato

1/2 cup cilantro, finely chopped
1/4 cup chopped jalapeño chiles
2 tablespoons cumin
2 tablespoons pepper
1 tablespoon sugar
1 tablespoon salt
Dash of Tabasco sauce
1 large avocado, chopped

Combine the salsa, black-eyed peas, hominy, bell pepper, onion, tomato, cilantro, jalapeño chiles, cumin, pepper, sugar, salt and Tabasco sauce in a large bowl and mix well. Chill, covered, in the refrigerator for 24 hours. Fold in the avocado just before serving. Serve with tortilla chips.

Serves 24

Corn Relish

2 (11-ounce) cans Mexicorn
1 cup sour cream
1 cup mayonnaise
3/4 cup medium-hot picante sauce
2 or 3 green onions, chopped

1 (4-ounce) can chopped green
  chiles, drained
8 ounces Cheddar cheese, shredded
2 packages corn chips

Place the Mexicorn in a colander and let drain for several minutes. Combine the sour cream, mayonnaise, picante sauce, green onions and green chiles in a bowl and mix well. Stir in the Cheddar cheese and Mexicorn. Chill, covered, for 4 to 10 hours. Serve with the corn chips.

Serves 12

Mango Salsa

2 mangoes, peeled, pitted and
  coarsely chopped
2 red onions, finely chopped
2 red bell peppers, chopped
1/2 cup cilantro, chopped
2 garlic cloves, minced

1 jalapeño chile, seeded and minced
1/2 cup orange juice
1/2 cup lime juice
1 tablespoon sugar
Salt and pepper to taste

Combine the mangoes, onions, bell peppers, cilantro, garlic, jalapeño chile, orange juice, lime juice, sugar, salt and pepper in a bowl and toss to mix well. Chill, covered, in the refrigerator for 4 to 6 hours. Serve with chips or atop grilled chicken.

Serves 6

Fruit Salsa

1 cup strawberries, finely chopped
1 orange, peeled and finely chopped
2 large kiwifruit, peeled and finely chopped
$^1/_2$ cup chopped fresh pineapple, or
    1 (8-ounce) can crushed pineapple, drained
$^1/_4$ cup thinly sliced green onions
$^1/_4$ cup finely chopped yellow bell pepper or green bell pepper
1 fresh jalapeño chile, seeded and chopped (optional)
1 tablespoon lime juice or lemon juice

Combine the strawberries, orange, kiwifruit, pineapple, green onions, bell pepper, jalapeño chile and lime juice in a bowl and stir to mix. Chill, covered, for 6 to 24 hours. Serve with Cinnamon Crisps (below). (Note: If you plan to chill the salsa for more than 6 hours, stir in the strawberries just before serving.)

Serves 8

CINNAMON CRISPS

Cut each of four 8-inch flour tortillas into eight triangles. Lightly coat both sides of each triangle with nonstick cooking spray. Lightly brush each side with a mixture of 1 tablespoon water and $^1/_2$ teaspoon vanilla extract. Sprinkle each side with a mixture of $^1/_4$ cup sugar and 1 teaspoon ground cinnamon. Place on a baking sheet and bake at 400 degrees for 8 to 10 minutes or until light brown.
Makes 32 triangles.

Orange Breakfast Nog

1 1/2 cups buttermilk
1/2 (6-ounce) can frozen orange
 juice concentrate (1/3 cup)

2 tablespoons brown sugar
1 teaspoon vanilla extract
2 or 3 large ice cubes

Process the buttermilk, orange juice concentrate, brown sugar and vanilla in a blender until smooth. Add the ice cubes one at a time through the opening in the blender lid, processing constantly until smooth and frothy.

Serves 2

Eggnog

6 egg yolks, beaten
2 cups milk
1/3 cup sugar
1 to 3 tablespoons light rum
1 to 3 tablespoons bourbon

1 teaspoon vanilla extract
1 cup heavy whipping cream
2 tablespoons sugar
Ground nutmeg

Beat the egg yolks, milk and 1/3 cup sugar in a large heavy saucepan until creamy and pale yellow. Cook over medium heat until the mixture just coats a metal spoon, stirring constantly. Remove from the heat. Place the saucepan in a large bowl filled with ice water and stir for 2 minutes. Stir in the rum, bourbon and vanilla. Cover and chill in the refrigerator for 24 hours.

Just before serving, beat the whipping cream and 2 tablespoons sugar in a mixing bowl until soft peaks form. Pour the chilled custard into a punch bowl. Fold in the whipped cream. Ladle into punch cups and sprinkle each serving with nutmeg.

Serves 10

Peanut Butter Martinis

1 jigger vodka
1 jigger Godiva chocolate liqueur
1 tablespoon peanut butter
1 scoop vanilla ice cream

Blend the vodka, chocolate liqueur, peanut butter and ice cream in a small pitcher. Pour into a martini glass.

Serves 1

Christmas Cranberry Punch

1 (12-ounce) can frozen cranberry juice concentrate, thawed
1 (46-ounce) can pineapple juice, chilled
1 (2-liter) bottle ginger ale, chilled

Combine the cranberry juice concentrate, pineapple juice and ginger ale in a punch bowl and blend well. Ladle into punch cups to serve. (Note: Champagne may be added for an alcoholic version.)

Serves 16

Summertime Slush

2 (12-ounce) cans frozen orange
   juice concentrate, thawed
1 (12-ounce) can frozen pink
   lemonade concentrate, thawed

2 to 4 bananas, sliced
1 (48-ounce) can pineapple juice
1 (2-liter) bottle Sprite, chilled

Prepare the orange juice concentrate in a pitcher according to the can directions. Prepare the lemonade concentrate in a pitcher according to the can directions. Mash the bananas in the pineapple juice in a pitcher. Combine the orange juice, lemonade and pineapple juice mixture in a large freezer container and blend well. Freeze until firm.

To serve, scrape the frozen punch mixture until slushy and place in serving cups. Pour the Sprite over the top of each serving.

Serves 16

Texas Twister

1 (32-ounce) can pineapple juice
1 (12-ounce) can frozen orange
   juice concentrate, thawed
2 1/2 concentrate cans water

14 ounces rum
8 ounces crème de banane liqueur
6 ounces Galliano liqueur
Cranberry juice cocktail

Blend the pineapple juice, orange juice concentrate, water, rum, cream de banana liqueur and Galliano liqueur in a 1-gallon pitcher. Serve over ice with a splash of cranberry juice cocktail.

Serves 12

Almond Tea

3 tablespoons instant tea granules
  or diet lemon tea granules
2 cups cold water
1 to 1 1/2 cups sugar
1 tablespoon vanilla extract

1 1/2 teaspoons almond extract
1 (12-ounce) can frozen
  lemonade concentrate
2 quarts water

Dissolve the tea granules in 2 cups cold water in a 1-gallon pitcher. Dissolve the sugar in the tea mixture. Add the vanilla, almond extract, frozen lemonade concentrate and 2 quarts water and stir to blend well. Serve over ice.

Serves 12

Russian Spiced Tea

2 teaspoons whole allspice
2 teaspoons whole cloves
5 cinnamon sticks
1 quart boiling water
1 1/2 cups sugar
6 small tea bags
1 quart boiling water

Juice of 4 oranges, or 2 cups
  prepared frozen orange
  juice concentrate
Juice of 4 lemons, or 1/2 cup
  bottled lemon juice
2 1/2 cups pineapple juice
Fresh mint
Orange and/or lemon slices

Place the allspice, cloves and cinnamon sticks in a large spice infuser or make a cloth bag to hold the spices. Place the spice infuser in 1 quart boiling water in a saucepan and boil for 10 minutes. Remove from the heat and remove the spice infuser. Dissolve the sugar in the hot liquid and let stand until cool.

Place the tea bags in 1 quart of boiling water in a saucepan and steep for 10 minutes. Pour the tea and spiced liquid into a 1-gallon pitcher. Add the orange juice, lemon juice and pineapple juice and blend well. Add enough additional water to make 1 gallon of liquid and blend well. Serve hot or over ice and garnish with fresh mint and orange and/or lemon slices.

Serves 16

Hot Buttered Rum

1 pound (4 sticks) butter, softened
1 (16-ounce) package brown sugar
1 (16-ounce) package confectioners' sugar
2 teaspoons ground cinnamon
2 teaspoons ground nutmeg
1 quart vanilla ice cream, softened
Rum
Whipped cream
Cinnamon sticks

Beat the butter, brown sugar, confectioners' sugar, ground cinnamon and nutmeg in a mixing bowl until light and fluffy. Add the ice cream and stir until well blended. Spoon into a 2-quart freezer container and freeze for up to 1 month.

For each serving, place 3 tablespoons of the frozen ice cream mixture and 1 jigger of rum in 1 cup boiling water and stir until smooth. Top with whipped cream and a cinnamon stick for stirring.

Serves 36

American Wassail

1 (14-ounce) can apple juice
1 (14-ounce) can pineapple juice
1 (6-ounce) can frozen orange juice concentrate, prepared
1 (6-ounce) can frozen lemonade concentrate, prepared
1 cup sugar
1/4 cup water
3 cinnamon sticks
1 teaspoon whole cloves

Combine the apple juice, pineapple juice, orange juice and lemonade in a large stockpot. Dissolve the sugar in the water in a small saucepan. Place the cinnamon sticks and cloves in a tea infuser or tie in a cheesecloth bag and add to the saucepan. Bring to a boil and boil for 5 minutes. Strain the hot liquid into the juice mixture. Bring to a boil and serve hot.

Serves 8

Helpful Hints

Appetizers & Beverages

*A*lways chill juices or sodas before adding to beverage recipes.

One lemon will yield $1/4$ cup of juice; one orange will yield $1/3$ cup of juice. This is helpful in making fresh orange juice or lemonade.

For non-alcoholic versions of your favorite drink, substitute orange juice for the rum.

Freeze the brewed coffee in ice cube trays to use in iced coffee drinks. As these cubes melt, they will not dilute the coffee drink.

To make decorative ice cubes, fill ice cube trays about two-thirds full with water and let freeze. Place decorations such as sprigs of mint, small slices of lime, lemon, or orange, or whole fresh strawberries in each ice cubicle. Gently add just enough water to cover and freeze until firm.

If your iced tea becomes cloudy, simply stir in a little boiling water and the tea will become clear again.

For a spicy aroma in your home, toss dried orange or lemon rinds into the fireplace.

Cheese will not dry out if it is wrapped in a cloth dampened with vinegar.

Sour cream will keep longer in the refrigerator if stored upside down so that air cannot enter the container.

To clean mushrooms, simply rub gently with a damp soft cloth.

For a change, serve dips in a hollowed-out red cabbage instead of a bowl.

For instant appetizers, serve popcorn heated with garlic butter, potato chips sprinkled with grated Parmesan cheese and broiled lightly, and pecan halves spread with sharp Cheddar cheese and joined together in pairs.

Serve blanched asparagus, fresh green beans, and strips of raw turnip along with the usual carrots and celery with dips.

Breads & Breakfast

"*If more of us valued food and cheer and song above hoarded gold,
it would be a merrier world.*"

—J. R. R. Tolkien

"*Never work before breakfast;
if you have to work before breakfast, eat your breakfast first.*"

—Josh Billings

"*We load up on oat bran in the morning so we'll live forever.
Then we spend the rest of the day living like there's no tomorrow.*"

—Lee Iacocca

"*Bread deals with living things,
with giving life, with growth, with the seed, the grain that nurtures.
It is not coincidence that we say bread is the staff of life.*"

—Lionel Poilane

Cream Biscuits

2 cups self-rising flour
1 tablespoon sugar
1 1/2 cups heavy whipping cream

Combine the flour, sugar and whipping cream in a bowl and stir until the mixture forms a ball. Knead on a lightly floured surface five to seven times. Gently pat or roll out the dough 1/2 inch thick. Cut with a 3-inch biscuit cutter. Place 1 inch apart on a well-greased baking sheet. Bake at 450 degrees for 10 minutes or until golden brown.

Serves 4

Almond Apricot Coffee Cake

1 cup (2 sticks) butter, softened
2 cups sugar
2 eggs
1 cup sour cream
1 teaspoon almond extract

2 cups all-purpose flour
1 teaspoon baking powder
1/4 teaspoon salt
1 (10-ounce) jar apricot preserves
1 1/2 cups sliced almonds

Cream the butter and sugar in a mixing bowl until light and fluffy. Add the eggs one at a time, beating well after each addition. Beat in the sour cream and almond extract. Add the flour, baking powder and salt gradually, stirring well after each addition. Spoon one-half of the batter into a greased and floured 9×13-inch baking pan. Dollop one-half of the apricot preserves over the batter and sprinkle with one-half of the almonds. Spread the remaining cake batter over the top. Dollop with the remaining preserves and sprinkle with the remaining almonds. Bake at 350 degrees for 45 minutes or until the coffee cake tests done.

(Variation: For Sour Cream Coffee Cake, use vanilla extract instead of the almond extract and use a mixture of 1 cup chopped pecans, 2 teaspoons ground cinnamon and 1/4 cup packed brown sugar for the almonds and apricot preserves. Spread the baked coffee cake with a mixture of 1 cup confectioners' sugar, 1 teaspoon vanilla extract and enough milk to make of a glaze consistency.)

Serves 12

Apple Cake

4 cups chopped peeled Granny
   Smith apples (3 or 4 large)
1 cup vegetable oil
2 cups sugar
2 eggs, lightly beaten
3 cups sifted all-purpose flour

1 teaspoon baking soda
1/2 teaspoon salt
1 teaspoon ground cinnamon
1 teaspoon ground nutmeg
1 teaspoon vanilla extract
1 cup chopped pecans (optional)

Mix the apples, oil and sugar in a large bowl and let stand for 1 hour. Add the eggs, flour, baking soda, salt, cinnamon, nutmeg and vanilla and mix well. Stir in the pecans. Grease a bundt pan with butter or nonstick cooking spray and coat the pan with additional sugar. Pour the batter into the prepared pan and bake at 350 degrees for 50 minutes. Remove the cake from the oven and cool completely before inverting onto a cake plate.

Serves 12

Banana Nut Bread

Cinnamon-sugar
1 cup (2 sticks) butter, softened
2 cups granulated sugar
4 eggs
2 1/2 cups all-purpose flour
2 teaspoons baking soda

1 teaspoon salt
2 teaspoons ground cinnamon
1/2 teaspoon ground cloves
6 large ripe bananas, cut into
   small pieces
1 cup nuts

Grease a bundt pan or two 5×9-inch loaf pans and coat with cinnamon-sugar. Cream the butter and granulated sugar in a mixing bowl until light and fluffy. Add the eggs and beat well. Add the flour, baking soda, salt, cinnamon and cloves and mix well. Stir in the bananas and nuts. Spoon into the bundt pan. Bake at 350 degrees for 50 minutes or until a wooden pick inserted in the center comes out clean. Cool in the pan for 10 minutes and invert onto a serving plate to cool completely. (Note: If loaf pans are used, thinly slice the bread and spread Cream Cheese Spread between the slices. To prepare, cream 8 ounces cream cheese, softened, and up to 2 cups confectioners' sugar together in a mixing bowl, depending on the sweetness and consistency desired.)

Serves 12

Zucchini Bread

2 cups all-purpose flour
1 teaspoon baking soda
2 teaspoons ground cinnamon
1 teaspoon salt
3 eggs
1 cup vegetable oil

2 cups sugar
1 tablespoon vanilla extract
2 cups shredded peeled zucchini
1 cup walnuts, chopped
1/2 cup golden raisins

Mix the flour, baking soda, cinnamon and salt together. Beat the eggs, oil, sugar and vanilla at medium-high speed in a mixing bowl until well mixed. Add the flour mixture and beat well. Add the zucchini, walnuts and raisins and stir until incorporated. Spoon into two greased 5×9-inch loaf pans. Bake at 350 degrees for 45 to 60 minutes or until the loaves test done. Cool in the pan for 10 minutes and invert onto a wire rack to cool completely.

Serves 16

Lemon Muffins

MUFFINS
1 (2-layer) package yellow
  cake mix
1 (4-ounce) package lemon
  instant pudding mix
4 eggs
3/4 cup vegetable oil

LEMON ICING
4 cups confectioners'
  sugar, sifted
1/3 cup fresh lemon juice
Zest of 1 lemon
3 tablespoons vegetable oil
3 tablespoons water

To prepare the muffins, combine the cake mix, pudding mix, eggs and oil in a mixing bowl and beat at medium speed for 2 minutes or until smooth. Pour into greased miniature muffin cups, filling each cup half full. Bake at 350 degrees for 12 minutes. Remove from the oven and invert onto a clean tea towel.

To prepare the icing, combine the confectioners' sugar, lemon juice, lemon zest, oil and water in a bowl and mix with a spoon until smooth.

To assemble, dip the warm muffins into the icing, covering as much of the muffin as possible, or spoon the icing over the warm muffins, turning to coat completely. Place on wire racks with waxed paper underneath to catch any drips. Let stand for 1 hour or until the icing is set. Store in a container with a tight-fitting lid.

Makes 5 dozen

Breakfast Bread

3/4 cup chopped green bell pepper
1/2 cup chopped red bell pepper
3/4 cup chopped onion
1 cup (2 sticks) margarine
3 (10-count) cans biscuits

8 ounces sliced bacon, cooked
  and crumbled
1/2 cup (2 ounces) shredded
  Parmesan cheese

Sauté the bell peppers and onion in the margarine in a skillet until tender. Separate the biscuit dough and cut each biscuit into quarters. Toss the biscuit quarters with the bacon, sautéed vegetables and Parmesan cheese in a bowl to coat. Place in a lightly greased bundt pan and bake at 350 degrees for 35 to 40 minutes or until golden brown. Cool in the pan for 10 minutes. Invert onto a serving plate and serve.

Serves 12

Onion Cheese Bread

1/2 cup chopped onion
3 tablespoons butter
1/2 cup milk
1 egg, lightly beaten
1 1/2 cups baking mix

1 cup (4 ounces) shredded sharp
  Cheddar cheese
1 tablespoon poppy seeds
1/2 cup thinly sliced onion pieces

Sauté the chopped onion in 1 tablespoon of the butter in a skillet until tender. Beat the milk and egg in a medium mixing bowl. Add the baking mix and stir just until moistened. Add the sautéed onion, one-half of the Cheddar cheese and one-half of the poppy seeds and mix well. Spoon into a greased 8-inch baking pan. Sprinkle with the remaining Cheddar cheese and poppy seeds. Sauté the thinly sliced onion pieces in 1 tablespoon of the remaining butter in a skillet until tender. Arrange over the batter. Melt the remaining 1 tablespoon butter and drizzle over the top. Bake at 400 degrees for 20 minutes.

Serves 8

CLASSIC CORN BREAD MUFFINS

Mix 2 cups cornmeal, 1 cup all-purpose flour, 1/4 cup sugar, 5 teaspoons baking powder and 1 teaspoon salt in a bowl. Add 3 cups buttermilk, 3 eggs and 1 cup vegetable oil and mix well. Pour into greased muffin cups, filling three-quarters full. Bake at 425 degrees for 15 to 20 minutes or until golden brown.
Makes 12 muffins.

Bran Rolls

2 cakes yeast
1 cup lukewarm water
1 cup shortening
3/4 cup sugar
1 1/2 teaspoons salt
1 cup 100% bran cereal
1 cup boiling water
2 eggs, beaten
6 1/2 cups all-purpose flour

Dissolve the yeast cakes in the lukewarm water. Place the shortening, sugar, salt and cereal in a large mixing bowl. Add the boiling water and stir until the shortening is melted. Let stand until the mixture is lukewarm. Add the eggs, yeast mixture and one-half of the flour and beat until smooth. Add the remaining flour and beat well. Cover the bowl and chill in the refrigerator for 8 to 10 hours or until ready to use. Shape the dough into rolls and place on a nonstick baking sheet. Let rise until doubled in bulk. Bake at 425 degrees for 12 to 15 minutes or until golden brown.

Makes 3 dozen

HONEY BUTTER

Cream 1/2 cup (1 stick) butter, softened, in a mixing bowl until light and fluffy. Add 1/4 cup honey gradually, beating constantly until blended. Stir in 2 teaspoons grated orange zest. Great served with hot baked rolls. Serves 12.

Orange Rolls

ROLLS
1 1/4 cups milk
1 cake yeast, or 1 envelope
   dry yeast
1/4 cup warm water
1/2 cup shortening
1/3 cup sugar
1 teaspoon salt
2 eggs, lightly beaten

1/4 cup orange juice
2 tablespoons grated orange zest
5 cups all-purpose flour
Softened butter

ORANGE ICING
1 cup confectioners' sugar
2 tablespoons orange juice
1 tablespoon grated orange zest

To prepare the rolls, scald the milk in a saucepan. Remove from the heat and cool to lukewarm. Dissolve the yeast in the warm water in a small bowl. Cream the shortening, sugar and salt in a mixing bowl until light and fluffy. Add the scalded milk and mix well. Add the yeast mixture, eggs, orange juice, orange zest and flour and mix well. Cover and let rise in a warm place until doubled in bulk. Punch the dough down and let rise in a warm place until doubled in bulk. Place the dough on a floured board and roll into a rectangle. Spread with butter and roll as for a jelly roll, sealing the edge and ends. Cut into 1-inch slices and place cut side down in a well-greased baking pan. Cover and let rise in a warm place until doubled in bulk. Bake at 375 degrees for 20 minutes or until golden brown.

To prepare the icing, combine the confectioners' sugar, orange juice and orange zest in a small bowl and mix until smooth. Spread over the warm rolls.

Makes 4 dozen

Baked Blueberry Pecan French Toast with Blueberry Syrup

FRENCH TOAST
1 (24-inch) baguette
6 eggs
2 cups half-and-half
1 cup whole milk or 2% milk
1/2 teaspoon freshly grated nutmeg
1 teaspoon vanilla extract
3/4 cup packed brown sugar
1 cup pecans
1 teaspoon unsalted butter

1/4 teaspoon salt
1 cup blueberries
  (about 12 ounces)
1/4 cup (1/2 stick) unsalted butter
1/4 cup packed brown sugar

BLUEBERRY SYRUP
1 cup blueberries
1/2 cup maple syrup
1 tablespoon lemon juice

To prepare the French toast, cut the baguette on the bias into twenty 1-inch slices. Arrange in a single layer in a buttered 9×13-inch baking dish. Whisk the eggs, half-and-half, milk, nutmeg, vanilla and 3/4 cup brown sugar in a large bowl. Pour evenly over the bread. Chill, covered, for 8 to 24 hours or until the bread absorbs all the liquid. Spread the pecans evenly in a shallow baking pan. Bake at 350 degrees on the middle oven rack for 8 minutes or until the pecans are toasted and fragrant. Add 1 teaspoon butter and the salt and toss to coat. Sprinkle the pecans and blueberries evenly over the bread mixture. Maintain the oven temperature. Melt 1/4 cup butter and 1/4 cup brown sugar together in a small saucepan, stirring constantly. Drizzle over the top of the blueberry layer. Bake for 40 minutes or until any liquid from the blueberries is bubbly.

To prepare the syrup, cook the blueberries and maple syrup in a saucepan over medium heat for 3 minutes or until the blueberries burst. Stir in the lemon juice. Serve over the hot French toast. (Note: The blueberry syrup may be strained through a sieve if you prefer to not have the blueberries in your syrup. The syrup may be made up to a day in advance and stored in the refrigerator. Reheat the syrup before serving.)

Serves 6

Pumpkin Pancakes with Apple Cinnamon Syrup

PANCAKES

1 egg
1 tablespoon vegetable oil
3/4 cup milk, or 1/2 cup yogurt
1/2 cup pumpkin purée
1 cup pancake mix
Ground cinnamon, ground cloves
    and ground ginger to taste

APPLE CINNAMON SYRUP

1 (12-ounce) can frozen apple
    juice concentrate
2 cups sugar
1 teaspoon ground cinnamon
2 cups (4 sticks) butter

To prepare the pancakes, combine the egg, oil, milk and pumpkin purée in a large mixing bowl and mix well. Mix the pancake mix, cinnamon, cloves and ginger together. Add to the pumpkin mixture and stir just enough to combine. Pour 1/4 cup at a time on a hot buttered griddle. Cook until brown on both sides, turning once.

To prepare the syrup, combine the apple juice concentrate, sugar, cinnamon and butter in a saucepan. Cook over low heat until melted and smooth, whisking frequently. Serve over the hot pancakes.

Makes 8 to 10 pancakes

FLAMING BLACKBERRIES

Place a 20-ounce package of frozen blackberries in a flat chafing dish and sprinkle with 1/4 cup sugar. Let stand until the blackberries are thawed. When ready to serve, heat the blackberries until the sugar is dissolved. Add 1/4 cup Grand Marnier and 2 to 3 tablespoons Cointreau and simmer over the flame until transparent. Pour 1/4 cup brandy evenly over the blackberries and heat, tipping the dish carefully so that the flame will ignite the brandy. This is fun to serve over pancakes or waffles for a special brunch party. Makes 4 cups.

Breakfast Bake

2 1/2 cups seasoned croutons
1 pound spicy sausage
4 eggs, beaten
2 1/4 cups milk
1 (10-ounce) can cream of
  chicken soup with herbs
1 (10-ounce) package frozen
  spinach, thawed and drained
1 (4-ounce) can mushroom
  pieces, drained

1 cup (4 ounces) shredded sharp
  Cheddar cheese
1 cup (4 ounces) shredded
  Monterey Jack cheese
1/2 teaspoon onion powder
1/2 teaspoon garlic powder
1/4 teaspoon dry mustard
Salt and pepper to taste

Spread the croutons in the bottom of a greased 9×13-inch baking dish. Brown the sausage in a skillet, stirring until crumbly; drain. Spread the sausage over the croutons. Mix the eggs and milk in a large bowl. Stir in the soup, spinach, mushrooms, Cheddar cheese, Monterey Jack cheese, onion powder, garlic powder, dry mustard, salt and pepper. Pour over the sausage layer and chill, covered, for 8 to 10 hours. Uncover and bake at 325 degrees for 50 to 55 minutes or until set.

Serves 6

Hawaiian Bread Casserole

1 (16-ounce) loaf Hawaiian
  bread, cut into cubes
2 cups (8 ounces) finely shredded
  Mexican four-cheese blend
8 ounces bacon, cooked and
  crumbled (8 slices)
8 eggs

2 1/2 cups milk
1 teaspoon dry mustard
1/2 teaspoon salt
1/2 teaspoon pepper
1/2 teaspoon Worcestershire sauce
Salsa or sliced tomatoes

Arrange the bread cubes in a lightly greased 9×13-inch baking dish. Sprinkle with the Mexican cheese and bacon. Whisk the eggs, milk, dry mustard, salt, pepper and Worcestershire sauce in a bowl. Pour over the layers, pressing down the bread cubes with a spoon to allow the bread cubes to soak up the liquid. Cover and chill for 8 hours. Let stand at room temperature for 30 minutes before baking. Bake at 350 degrees for 35 minutes or until set and golden. Serve with salsa or sliced tomatoes.

Serves 8 to 10

Ham and Asparagus Breakfast Casserole

8 ounces fresh asparagus, trimmed

1 bell pepper, chopped

1 onion, chopped

$1/4$ cup ($1/2$ stick) margarine

1 loaf French bread, cut into cubes

1 cup chopped ham

2 cups (8 ounces) shredded Cheddar cheese

8 eggs

$2 1/2$ cups milk

$1/3$ cup honey

$1/2$ tablespoon salt

$1/2$ tablespoon pepper

Sauté the asparagus, bell pepper and onion in the margarine in a skillet for 3 to 5 minutes or until tender. Layer the bread, ham, 1 cup of the Cheddar cheese and the sautéed vegetables in a greased 9×13-inch baking dish. Beat the eggs, milk, honey, salt and pepper in a bowl until smooth. Pour over the layers and sprinkle with the remaining 1 cup Cheddar cheese. Chill, covered, for 8 to 10 hours. Uncover and bake at 350 degrees for 40 to 45 minutes or until set.

Serves 12

Frittata

6 eggs

$1/8$ teaspoon pepper

$1/4$ cup chopped onion

1 garlic clove, minced

1 tablespoon butter

$3/4$ cup chopped cooked vegetables or meat

2 tablespoons grated Parmesan cheese or Romano cheese

Beat the eggs and pepper in a bowl until smooth. Sauté the onion and garlic in the butter in a 10-inch broiler-proof skillet until tender. Stir in the vegetables. Pour the egg mixture into the skillet. Cook over medium heat, running a spatula around the edge of the skillet as the mixture sets and lifting the egg mixture so the uncooked portion flows underneath. Continue to cook and lift the edge until the egg mixture is almost set. The surface should still be moist. Broil 4 to 5 inches from the heat source for 1 to 2 minutes or until the top is set. Sprinkle with the Parmesan cheese. Cut into wedges and serve immediately.

Serves 3

Hash Brown Quiche

1 (16-ounce) package frozen hash
   brown potatoes, thawed
1/2 cup (1 stick) butter, melted
1 cup (4 ounces) shredded
   Cheddar cheese
1 cup (4 ounces) shredded
   Swiss cheese

1 cup chopped ham or
   crumbled bacon
6 eggs
1 1/2 cups milk
1 teaspoon salt

Line a 9×13-inch baking dish 1/2 inch thick with the hash brown potatoes.
Brush with the butter. Bake at 425 degrees for 25 minutes. Remove from the
oven and reduce the oven temperature to 375 degrees. Layer the Cheddar cheese,
Swiss cheese and ham in the prepared dish. Beat the eggs, milk and salt in a
bowl until smooth and pour over the top. Bake for 30 to 40 minutes or until
set. (Note: You may spray the hash brown potatoes with buttered cooking
spray instead of using the melted butter.)

Serves 8

Chile-Cheese Grits

5 3/4 cups water
1 1/3 cups quick-cooking grits
1/2 cup (1 stick) butter, melted
4 cups (16 ounces) shredded
   medium-sharp Cheddar cheese
3 eggs

1 mild green chile, chopped
1 or 2 garlic cloves, minced
2 teaspoons salt
2 teaspoons Tabasco sauce
1/2 teaspoon paprika

Bring the water to a boil in a large saucepan. Stir in the grits gradually, making
sure the water remains at a boil. Cook for 5 to 7 minutes or until thickened,
stirring constantly. Cover and remove from the heat.

Combine the butter, Cheddar cheese, eggs, green chile, garlic,
salt and Tabasco sauce in a medium mixing bowl and mix well.
Stir in the grits. Pour into a generously greased 3-quart baking
dish and sprinkle with the paprika. Bake at 325 degrees for 30 to
40 minutes or until puffed and light brown.

Serves 12

HELPFUL HINTS

Breads & Breakfast

*W*hen baking bread, place a small dish of water in the oven with the bread to help keep the crust from getting too hard or too brown.

Nut breads are better if stored 24 hours before serving.

When baking bread, you will get a finer texture if you use milk; water will make a coarser texture.

To make lighter muffins, place the greased muffin cups into the oven for a few minutes before adding the batter.

Fill muffin cups easily and neatly by using an ice cream scoop.

To test the freshness of an egg, place it in a large bowl of cold water. If it floats, do not use it.

Dip bacon in cold water to prevent shrinkage and shriveling when frying.

Flouring sausage patties on both sides before cooking gives them a crunchy crust and helps keep the grease from splattering.

To thicken gravy in a hurry, add some instant potatoes to the gravy.

When making gravy, brown the all-purpose flour well before adding the liquid. This helps prevents lumpy gravy.

For lighter pancakes, replace the liquid in the batter with club soda.

Keep waffles warm until ready to serve by placing them on a rack set on a baking sheet in a 350-degree oven.

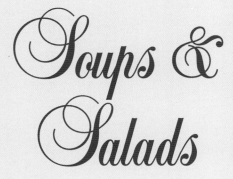

Soups & Salads

"Worries go down better with soup."

—Jewish Proverb

"As the days grow short, some faces grow long. But not mine. Every autumn, when the wind turns cold and darkness comes early, I am suddenly happy. It's time to start making soup again."

—Leslie Newman

"I don't think America will have really made it until we have our own salad dressing. Until then, we're stuck behind the French, Italians, Russians, and Caesarians."

—Pat McNelis

Squash and Poblano Chile Soup

1 butternut squash
1 yellow onion, chopped
3 tablespoons olive oil
4 to 6 cups chicken stock or vegetable stock
2 poblano chiles
Juice of 1 lime
Salt and pepper to taste
3 tablespoons chopped cilantro
1/2 cup sour cream
12 to 16 cilantro leaves
6 to 8 lime slices

Cut the neck off the squash. Place the squash cut side down on a cutting board and slice the skin off with a sharp knife following the contour of the squash. Repeat for the neck of the squash. Cut the peeled squash into 1-inch chunks. Steam the squash in a steamer until soft.

Sauté the onion in the hot olive oil in a 3- to 4-quart stockpot until translucent. Add the steamed squash and 4 cups of the stock. Simmer over low heat. Roast the poblano chiles over a gas flame or broil on a rack in a broiler pan until the skins are lightly charred. Place the roasted poblano chiles in a bowl and cover with plastic wrap. Let sweat for 15 minutes. Peel the poblano chiles and remove the seeds. Chop the poblano chiles and add to the soup. Simmer for 15 minutes. Purée the soup with an immersion blender in the stockpot or purée in batches in a blender, adding additional stock if needed for a thinner consistency. Season with the lime juice, salt and pepper. Stir in the chopped cilantro just before serving. Ladle into soup bowls and garnish each serving with a tablespoon of sour cream, a couple of cilantro leaves and a slice of lime.

Serves 6 to 8

Red River Tortilla Soup

$1^1/2$ quarts water
4 beef bouillon cubes
2 chicken bouillon cubes
10 corn tortillas
1 onion, chopped
2 garlic cloves, finely chopped
1 jalapeño chile, seeded and
    finely chopped
2 tablespoons vegetable oil
$^1/2$ cup tomato sauce
1 teaspoon salt
1 teaspoon cumin

1 teaspoon chili powder
1 teaspoon Worcestershire sauce
1 cup chopped cooked chicken
2 tomatoes, peeled and chopped
$^1/2$ cup vegetable oil
2 cups (8 ounces) shredded
    Monterey Jack cheese
1 avocado, peeled, seeded
    and chopped
Chopped fresh cilantro leaves
Lime wedges (optional)
Hot pepper sauce (optional)

Combine the water, bouillon cubes and 3 of the tortillas in a small Dutch oven. Bring to a boil and reduce the heat. Simmer for 1 hour, stirring occasionally to break up the tortillas. Strain the broth through a fine mesh sieve into a 2-quart glass measure, pressing the tortillas through the sieve using the back of a wooden spoon. Add enough water to the strained mixture to measure 6 cups.

Sauté the onion, garlic and jalapeño chile in 2 tablespoons oil in the Dutch oven for 3 minutes. Stir in the tortilla broth mixture, tomato sauce, salt, cumin, chili powder and Worcestershire sauce. Bring to a boil and reduce the heat. Cover and simmer for 1 hour. Stir in the chicken and tomatoes. Simmer for 10 minutes.

Cut the remaining tortillas into $^1/2$×2-inch strips. Fry in $^1/2$ cup oil in a heavy skillet until crisp. Remove to paper towels to drain.

To serve, place several of the fried tortilla strips in the bottom of each soup bowl and top with 2 tablespoons Monterey Jack cheese and 1 tablespoon avocado. Ladle the soup into the prepared bowls and sprinkle with the remaining tortilla pieces and cheese. Garnish with cilantro leaves. Serve with lime wedges and hot sauce.

Makes $1^1/2$ quarts

Crab and Corn Chowder

4 potatoes, finely chopped
1 white onion, chopped
1/2 cup (1 stick) butter, melted
Tony Chachere's Cajun seasoning
1 (15-ounce) can
  sweet corn, drained

1 (2-ounce) jar chopped
  pimento, drained
1 pint half-and-half or milk
8 ounces crab meat, drained and
  flaked, or 2 packages lump
  crab meat

Sauté the potatoes and onion in the melted butter in a large sauté pan or stockpot until almost tender. Season with Cajun seasoning. Add the corn, pimento and half-and-half and stir to mix. Cook until heated through. Stir in the crab meat just before serving.

Serves 4 to 6

Chilled Marinated Shrimp Soup

1 pound uncooked large shrimp,
  peeled and deveined
Salt to taste
1 1/4 cups fresh orange juice
1 cup fresh lime juice
1 cup chopped seeded tomatoes
1/4 onion, sliced
1/4 cup ketchup

2 1/2 tablespoons brown sugar
2 jalapeño chiles, seeded
  and minced
2 teaspoons Worcestershire sauce
1 1/2 teaspoons Pickapeppa Sauce
Pepper to taste
1 tomato, seeded and chopped
Fresh lime slices

Cook the shrimp in boiling salted water in a medium saucepan for 1 minute or until the shrimp turn pink; drain. Combine the orange juice, lime juice, 1 cup chopped tomatoes, onion, ketchup, brown sugar, jalapeño chiles, Worcestershire sauce and Pickapeppa Sauce in a large glass bowl and mix well. Add the shrimp. Cover and marinate in the refrigerator for 8 to 10 hours. Season the soup with salt and pepper. Ladle into soup bowls and garnish with chopped tomato and lime slices.

Serves 6

Gazpacho

3 or 4 tomatoes, peeled and chopped
3 large cucumbers, peeled, seeded
  and chopped
1 large sweet onion, chopped
1 large green bell pepper, chopped
$1/3$ cup olive oil
$1/3$ cup red wine vinegar
$1/4$ teaspoon Tabasco sauce

$1 1/2$ teaspoons salt, or to taste
1 (4-ounce) jar pimentos, chopped
$2 1/2$ cups tomato juice
  (20 ounces)
1 cup vegetable juice cocktail
  (8 ounces)
Croutons
2 small avocados, sliced

Process the tomatoes, 2 of the cucumbers, $3/4$ of the onion, $3/4$ of the bell pepper, the olive oil, wine vinegar, Tabasco sauce, salt and pimentos in a food processor until blended. Combine the blended tomato mixture, tomato juice and vegetable juice cocktail in a large bowl. Stir in the remaining cucumber, onion and bell pepper. Chill in the refrigerator until ready to serve.

To serve, ladle the chilled soup into soup bowls and top with the croutons and avocados.

Serves 6

Wild Mushroom Bisque

4 cups dehydrated mushrooms
2 cups white wine
1 shallot, finely chopped
2 garlic cloves, finely chopped

1 tablespoon clarified butter
3 cups (or more) chicken stock
Salt and white pepper to taste
2 cups heavy whipping cream

Soak the mushrooms in the wine in a bowl for 8 to 10 hours. Process the mushrooms and wine in a food processor until smooth. Sauté the shallot and garlic in the clarified butter in a 2-quart saucepan until golden brown. Add the mushroom mixture and chicken stock and simmer for 1 hour, stirring constantly to prevent burning and adding additional chicken stock if needed. Season with salt and white pepper.

Whip the whipping cream at high speed in a cold mixing bowl until soft peaks form. Purée the soup with a bur mixer or blender. Strain the soup through a fine mesh strainer or cheesecloth into a saucepan. Heat the soup to the desired temperature. Add the whipped cream and mix until frothy. Ladle into soup bowls and serve with Swiss cheese croutons.

Makes 8 cups

Fully Loaded Potato Soup

4 or 5 slices bacon
1 yellow onion, chopped
2 or 3 baking potatoes, peeled and
    cut into cubes
3 to 4 cups chicken broth
1/4 cup cream, half-and-half
    or milk

Salt and pepper to taste
Sour cream
Chopped chives
Shredded Cheddar cheese

Cook the bacon in a large saucepan until almost crisp. Remove the bacon to paper towels to drain. Drain the saucepan, leaving a small amount of the bacon drippings. Sauté the onion in the reserved bacon drippings in the saucepan until tender. Add the potatoes and sauté briefly. Add enough chicken broth to cover. Bring to a boil and cook until the potatoes are tender. Crumble the bacon and return to the saucepan. Stir in the cream and season with salt and pepper. Cook until heated through. Do not boil. Ladle into soup bowls and dollop each serving with sour cream. Sprinkle with chives and Cheddar cheese.

Serves 6

Lentil Soup

1 yellow onion, finely chopped
3 tablespoons olive oil
1 carrot, peeled and finely chopped
2 garlic cloves, sliced
2 cups French lentils
4 to 6 cups chicken stock, vegetable
    stock or water
2 or 3 bay leaves

2 or 3 teaspoons curry powder
Salt and pepper to taste
1 apple, chopped
1/4 cup raisins
2 tablespoons chopped cilantro
Juice of 1 lemon
1/2 cup plain yogurt

Sauté the onion in the olive oil in a 3- to 4-quart stockpot until translucent. Add the carrot and sauté for 5 minutes. Add the garlic, lentils and 4 cups of the chicken stock. Bring to a simmer. Add the bay leaves and curry powder. Simmer over low heat for 45 minutes or until the lentils are soft, adding additional chicken stock as needed. Season with salt and pepper. Discard the bay leaves. Mix the apple, raisins, cilantro and lemon juice in a bowl. Ladle the soup into soup bowls and add a scoop of the apple mixture. Top each with about 1 tablespoon yogurt.

Serves 4 to 6

Chinese Chicken Soup

6 cups chicken broth

1 whole chicken breast, cooked, skinned, boned and thinly sliced

1 (8-ounce) can sliced water chestnuts, drained

4 ounces fresh mushrooms, sliced, or

    1 (4-ounce) can sliced mushrooms

$1/2$ cup finely chopped onion

$1/4$ cup finely chopped green bell pepper

$1/4$ cup finely chopped celery

$1/4$ cup grated carrots

1 (4-ounce) jar chopped pimentos

1 teaspoon cornstarch

2 tablespoons cold water

1 tablespoon cooking sherry (optional)

Salt to taste

$1/4$ teaspoon Oriental sesame oil (optional)

Bring the chicken broth to a boil in a large saucepan. Add the chicken, water chestnuts, mushrooms, onion, bell pepper, celery, carrots and pimentos. Return to a boil and reduce the heat to low. Simmer for 5 to 6 minutes or until heated through. Blend the cornstarch with the cold water in a small bowl. Stir the cornstarch mixture and sherry into the soup. Cook over medium heat until slightly thickened, stirring constantly. Season with salt. Stir in the sesame oil, which will give the soup a pleasant nut-like flavor. Ladle into soup bowls and serve piping hot. (Note: This soup doesn't cure a cold, but it makes you feel better while you are recuperating. It may be frozen for later use.)

Serves 6 to 8

HOMEMADE CROUTONS

Cut 2 slices of French or Italian bread into 1-inch cubes. Combine the bread cubes, $1/4$ cup olive oil, 1 or 2 garlic cloves, minced, 1 teaspoon dried basil, 1 teaspoon dried thyme and 1 teaspoon dried oregano in a large bowl and toss to evenly coat. Spread the bread cubes on a baking sheet and bake at 400 degrees for 15 to 20 minutes or until golden brown. Serves 4.

Pear Soup

1 cinnamon stick
8 whole cloves
1 bay leaf
2 peppercorns
1 (1-inch) piece of gingerroot
6 ripe pears, peeled and chopped
1 1/3 cups white wine
1 (3-inch) piece of lemon grass
1/4 cup sugar
2 cups water
12 gingersnap cookies or thin shortbread biscuits
Fresh raspberries
Sprigs of fresh mint

Place the cinnamon stick, cloves, bay leaf, peppercorns and gingerroot in the center of a piece of cheesecloth. Wrap the cheesecloth around the spices and tie with string to secure. Bring the spice sachet, pears, wine, lemon grass, sugar and water to a boil in a large saucepan and reduce the heat. Simmer for 25 to 30 minutes or until the pears are tender but not mushy. Remove from the heat. Discard the sachet and lemon grass. Purée the pear mixture in a blender. Pour into a container and chill, covered, in the refrigerator.

To serve, pour the soup into cordials. Serve the cookies alongside the soup or crumble coarsely and sprinkle on top. Garnish each serving with fresh raspberries and a sprig of mint.

Serves 6

Strawberry Soup

1 cup fresh strawberries
1 cup orange juice
$1/4$ cup honey
$1/4$ cup sour cream

$1/2$ cup sweet white wine (optional)
Whipped cream
Sliced fresh strawberries
Mint leaves

Rinse the strawberries and remove the caps. Process the strawberries, orange juice, honey, sour cream and wine in a blender until puréed. Pour into a container and chill, covered, in the refrigerator.

To serve, stir the chilled soup and pour into small cordials. Garnish each serving with whipped cream, sliced strawberries and mint leaves. (Note: You may use frozen strawberries instead of the fresh. You may substitute blueberries or raspberries for the strawberries.)

Serves 6

Merry Berry Salad

1 (6-ounce) package
   raspberry gelatin
$1^1/2$ cups boiling water
3 (10-ounce) packages
   frozen raspberries
1 teaspoon lemon juice

2 cups sour cream
1 (6-ounce) package cherry gelatin
1 cup boiling water
1 (13-ounce) can crushed pineapple
1 (16-ounce) can whole
   cranberry sauce

Dissolve the raspberry gelatin in $1^1/2$ cups boiling water in a bowl. Add the frozen raspberries and lemon juice and stir until the raspberries are thawed. Pour into a 9×13-inch glass dish and chill until firm.

Cover the congealed layer with the sour cream. Dissolve the cherry gelatin in 1 cup boiling water in a bowl. Stir in the pineapple and cranberry sauce. Chill until slightly thickened. Spoon over the sour cream layer. Chill until firm.

Serves 15 to 18

The Falls' Field Green Salad with Spicy Pecans

THE FALLS' VINAIGRETTE

2/3 cup sugar

1 teaspoon dry mustard

1 teaspoon salt

3 tablespoons apple cider vinegar

2/3 cup white vinegar

4 1/2 teaspoons onion juice

2 tablespoons Worcestershire sauce

1 cup vegetable oil

SALAD

4 cups mixed field greens

2 green onions, chopped

1 cup crumbled blue cheese

1 Granny Smith apple, chopped

1/4 cup Spicy Pecans, coarsely chopped (below)

To prepare the vinaigrette, combine the sugar, dry mustard, salt, apple cider vinegar and white vinegar in a bowl and whisk until the sugar is dissolved. Whisk in the onion juice and Worcestershire sauce. Add the oil in a fine stream, whisking constantly until blended.

To prepare the salad, combine the mixed field greens, green onions, blue cheese, apple and Spicy Pecans in a salad bowl and toss to mix. Add the vinaigrette and toss to coat.

Serves 8

SPICY PECANS

Melt 3 tablespoons butter in a saucepan. Add 2 tablespoons Worcestershire sauce, 1 teaspoon salt, 1/4 teaspoon cayenne pepper, 1/4 teaspoon garlic powder and 1/4 teaspoon cinnamon and mix well. Add 2 1/2 cups pecan halves and stir until coated. Add 1 tablespoon chili powder and toss to coat. Spread the pecan mixture in a shallow baking pan. Bake at 300 degrees for 30 minutes, stirring every 10 minutes. Makes 2 1/2 cups.

Romaine with Dried Cranberries and Toasted Ramen Noodles

SWEET-AND-SOUR VINAIGRETTE
1 cup vegetable oil
1 cup sugar
1/2 cup red wine vinegar
1 tablespoon soy sauce

SALAD
1 (3-ounce) package ramen noodles
1/4 cup (1/2 stick) butter

1 cup chopped walnuts
2 heads romaine, rinsed, dried and
    chopped, or 2 packages pre-
    washed chopped romaine
1 small head fresh broccoli,
    finely chopped
1 bunch green onions, chopped
1 package sweetened cherry-flavored
    dried cranberries

To prepare the vinaigrette, whisk the oil, sugar, wine vinegar and soy sauce in a bowl. Chill, covered, in the refrigerator. (The flavor of the vinaigrette is enhanced if made up to a day ahead of serving.)

To prepare the salad, crush the ramen noodles, reserving the seasoning packet for another purpose. Melt the butter in a skillet over medium heat. Add the crushed noodles and walnuts and sauté until toasted and light brown. Spread on waxed paper or paper towels to cool. Combine the romaine, broccoli and green onions in a salad bowl and toss to mix. Sprinkle with the dried cranberries and ramen noodle mixture. Whisk the vinaigrette to blend. Add about 1 cup of the vinaigrette to the salad and toss to coat. Store the remaining vinaigrette in the refrigerator. (Note: For a nice presentation, mix the lettuce, broccoli and green onions and place in a large bowl. Arrange the cranberries in a 3- to 4-inch circle in the center. Sprinkle the toasted walnuts around the circle of the cranberries. Sprinkle the toasted ramen noodles around the circle of walnuts. Toss with the vinaigrette just before serving. If you are making the salad for a large group, add an additional head of romaine or a different kind of lettuce, add an additional half package of dried cranberries and double the amounts of the ramen noodles, walnuts and broccoli.)

Serves 10 to 12

Mixed Greens with Mandarin Oranges and Strawberries

MANDARIN SALAD DRESSING
1/2 cup canola oil
1/2 cup sugar
1/4 cup red wine vinegar
1 1/2 teaspoons soy sauce

SALAD
1 package pre-washed plain
    lettuce pieces
2 packages pre-washed romaine

4 green onions, cut into 1-inch
    pieces (optional)
1 cup thinly diagonally sliced celery
1 (15-ounce) can mandarin
    oranges, drained
1 quart fresh strawberries, sliced
1/2 to 1 cup sliced
    honey-roasted almonds

To prepare the dressing, whisk the canola oil, sugar, wine vinegar and soy sauce in a bowl until the sugar is dissolved.

To prepare the salad, combine the plain lettuce, romaine, green onions, celery, mandarin oranges and strawberries in a salad bowl. Add the dressing and toss to coat. Sprinkle with the almonds. (Note: You may roast your own almonds instead of purchasing honey-roasted almonds. To roast, heat 1 tablespoon sugar in a skillet and add 2 packages of sliced almonds. Sauté until the almonds are coated with the sugar and are light brown. Remove from the skillet and spread on waxed paper or foil to cool.)

Serves 10 to 12

POSADA SALAD DRESSING

For a delicious dressing for tossed salad greens, process 1 onion, chopped, 3 garlic cloves, 2 cups vegetable oil, 3/4 cup apple cider vinegar, 1/4 cup water, 3 tablespoons sugar, 1 tablespoon salt, 1 teaspoon chopped parsley, 1 teaspoon chopped celery, 1/4 teaspoon mustard, 1/4 teaspoon paprika and 1/8 teaspoon pepper in a blender until blended. Makes 2 cups.

Yummy Mandarin Spinach Salad

8 cups baby spinach leaves
1/2 red onion, sliced and separated
   into rings
1 (11-ounce) can mandarin
   oranges, drained
1 1/2 cups sweetened
   dried cranberries

1 cup honey-roasted sliced almonds
1 cup crumbled feta cheese
1 cup balsamic vinaigrette,
   or to taste
Dash of pepper (optional)

Divide the spinach among six salad plates. Top each with the red onion, mandarin oranges, dried cranberries, sliced almonds and feta cheese in the order listed. Drizzle with the vinaigrette and sprinkle with pepper.

Serves 6

Mixed Salad Greens with Honey Mustard Dressing

HONEY MUSTARD DRESSING

6 tablespoons vegetable oil
1 garlic clove, minced
2 tablespoons honey
2 tablespoons cider vinegar
2 tablespoons coarse grain mustard
1 teaspoon pepper
2 tablespoons toasted sesame seeds

SALAD

1 bunch spinach, torn into pieces
1 bunch romaine or leaf
   lettuce, torn into pieces
3 green onions, sliced
6 slices bacon, cooked crisp
   and crumbled
2 avocados, sliced

To prepare the dressing, whisk the oil, garlic, honey, cider vinegar, mustard and pepper in a bowl until blended. Stir in the sesame seeds.

To prepare the salad, combine the spinach, romaine, green onions and bacon in a salad bowl and toss to mix. Add the dressing and toss to coat. Top with the avocado slices.

Serves 8

Greek Salad

GREEK SALAD DRESSING
6 tablespoons olive oil
1 teaspoon dried oregano
Juice of 1 lemon
Freshly ground pepper to taste

SALAD
1 head romaine, rinsed, dried and
   torn into pieces

1 red onion, chopped
1 (6-ounce) can pitted black
   olives, cut into halves
2 red bell peppers, chopped
6 Roma tomatoes, chopped
1 English cucumber, thinly sliced
1 (4-ounce) package crumbled
   tomato basil feta cheese

To prepare the dressing, whisk the olive oil, oregano, lemon juice and pepper in a bowl.

To prepare the salad, combine the romaine, onion, olives, bell peppers, tomatoes, cucumber and feta cheese in a bowl and toss to mix. Pour the dressing over the salad and toss to coat.

Serves 14 to 18

Make-Ahead Romaine Salad

Juice of 2 lemons
2 large Haas avocados, chopped
6 green onions, sliced
2 heaping teaspoons
   Beau Monde seasoning

$1/2$ to $3/4$ cup freshly grated or
   shredded Parmesan cheese
2 heads romaine
$3/4$ cup corn oil
Salt to taste

Place the lemon juice, avocados, green onions, Beau Monde seasoning and one-half of the Parmesan cheese in a large deep salad bowl. Do not mix. Tear the romaine into bite-size pieces and place on top. Sprinkle with the remaining Parmesan cheese. Chill, covered, for 6 to 8 hours.

To serve, drizzle with the corn oil and sprinkle with the salt. Toss the salad to mix.

Serves 4 to 6

Chicken Gorgonzola Salad

6 cups torn romaine

12 ounces boneless skinless chicken breasts, baked and cooled

1 Braeburn apple or Gala apple, cored and sliced

1/2 cup chopped red onion

1/4 cup pecan pieces

1/2 cup crumbled Gorgonzola cheese

1/2 cup thawed frozen apple juice concentrate

1/4 cup balsamic vinegar

1 1/2 teaspoons sesame oil

Place 1 1/2 cups romaine on each of four salad plates. Top evenly with the chicken. Sprinkle with the apple slices, onion, pecans and Gorgonzola cheese. Whisk the apple juice concentrate, balsamic vinegar and sesame oil in a bowl until blended. Spoon about 3 tablespoons of the dressing over each salad.

Serves 4

Curried Chicken Salad

3 or 4 boneless skinless chicken breasts, stewed and coarsely chopped

1 cup chopped celery

1 pound seedless grapes, cut into halves

1 (10-ounce) can sliced water chestnuts, drained

1 1/2 cups slivered almonds, toasted

1 1/2 cups mayonnaise

1 teaspoon curry powder

1 tablespoon soy sauce

1 tablespoon lemon juice

8 lettuce cups

1 avocado, cut into 8 slices

1 cup pineapple tidbits

Combine the chicken, celery, grapes, water chestnuts and almonds in a large bowl and toss to mix well. Blend the mayonnaise, curry powder, soy sauce and lemon juice in a bowl. Fold into the chicken mixture. Marinate, covered, in the refrigerator for 8 to 10 hours.

To serve, spoon the chicken salad into the lettuce cups. Garnish with the avocado slices and pineapple tidbits.

Serves 8

Shrimp Arnaud

6 tablespoons olive oil
2 tablespoons vinegar
1 tablespoon horseradish mustard
1 1/2 teaspoons paprika
1 1/2 tablespoons chopped green
   onion tops
1/4 cup chopped celery
1 tablespoon chopped parsley

1 tablespoon grated onion
Salt and pepper to taste
2 pounds boiled shrimp, peeled
   and deveined
4 cups shredded lettuce
2 tomatoes, cut into quarters
2 hard-cooked eggs, sliced

Blend the olive oil, vinegar, mustard and paprika in a large container. Stir in the green onion tops, celery, parsley, onion, salt and pepper. Add the shrimp and stir to coat. Marinate, covered, in the refrigerator for at least 2 hours before serving.

To serve, divide the lettuce among eight salad plates. Spoon the shrimp over the top and garnish with the tomato quarters and hard-cooked egg slices.

Serves 8

Broccoli Salad

2 to 3 broccoli crowns
1 (8-ounce) can water chestnuts,
   drained and chopped
1 cup chopped celery
1/2 cup chopped red onion
1/2 cup raisins

8 ounces bacon, crisp-cooked
   and crumbled
1 cup mayonnaise
1/3 cup sugar
1 tablespoon vinegar or lemon juice

Separate the broccoli into florets and place in a large bowl. Add the water chestnuts, celery, onion, raisins and bacon and mix well. Whisk the mayonnaise, sugar and vinegar in a bowl. Pour over the broccoli mixture and toss to coat. Chill, covered, until ready to serve.

Serves 6

Hot and Spicy Coleslaw

6 slices bacon
1 large onion, chopped
1 green bell pepper, chopped
1 (16-ounce) package finely
 shredded coleslaw

1/4 cup chili powder
Salt to taste
1 (10-ounce) can tomatoes with
 green chiles

Cook the bacon in a large skillet until crisp. Remove the bacon to paper towels to drain, reserving the drippings in the skillet. Crumble the bacon.

Sauté the onion and bell pepper in the reserved drippings until tender. Add the shredded coleslaw and cook until limp but not soft. Sprinkle with the chili powder and salt. Stir in the tomatoes with green chiles. Simmer until heated through. Serve immediately with the crumbled bacon on top.

Serves 6

Oriental Cabbage Slaw

1 (3-ounce) package chicken-
 flavored ramen noodles
1 (10-ounce) package
 shredded cabbage
2 tablespoons sunflower seeds
1/2 cup slivered almonds
4 green onions, finely chopped

4 slices bacon, cooked and crumbled
 (optional)
1/2 cup vegetable oil
1/3 cup white vinegar
2 tablespoons sugar
1/4 teaspoon pepper

Crumble the ramen noodles, reserving the seasoning packet. Combine the cabbage, sunflower seeds, almonds and green onions in a large bowl and toss to mix. Sprinkle the bacon and crumbled ramen noodles over the top.

Whisk the oil, white vinegar, sugar, pepper and the contents of the reserved seasoning packet in a bowl until blended. Pour over the cabbage mixture and toss to coat. Chill in the refrigerator for a few minutes before serving.

Serves 4 to 6

Panzanella

DRESSING FOR PANZANELLA
1/2 cup good-quality olive oil
3 tablespoons Champagne vinegar
1 teaspoon finely chopped garlic
1/2 teaspoon Dijon mustard
1/2 teaspoon kosher salt
1/4 teaspoon freshly ground pepper

SALAD
1 small loaf French bread, cut into 1-inch pieces (6 cups)
1 teaspoon kosher salt
3 tablespoons (or more) good-quality olive oil
2 large ripe tomatoes, cut into 1-inch pieces
1 cucumber, seeded and sliced 1/2 inch thick
1 red bell pepper, seeded and cut into 1-inch pieces
1 yellow bell pepper, seeded and cut into 1-inch pieces
1/2 red onion, cut into halves and thinly sliced
20 large basil leaves, coarsely chopped
3 tablespoons capers
Salt and pepper to taste

To prepare the dressing, whisk the olive oil, vinegar, garlic, Dijon mustard, kosher salt and pepper in a bowl until blended.

To prepare the salad, season the bread with the kosher salt. Sauté in the hot olive oil in a sauté pan over low to medium heat for 10 minutes or until brown, adding additional olive oil if needed. Combine the tomatoes, cucumber, bell peppers, onion, basil and capers in a large salad bowl and mix well. Add the bread cubes and dressing and toss to coat. Season liberally with salt and pepper. Serve immediately or let the salad stand for 30 minutes for the flavors to blend.

Serves 4 to 6

Olive Pasta Salad

GARLIC VINAIGRETTE
3 garlic cloves
3/4 cup olive oil
1/3 cup red wine vinegar
Coarsely ground pepper

SALAD
8 ounces pasta, cooked and drained
1/2 cup chopped green olives
1/2 cup black olives, sliced
1 cup sliced celery
1 cup grated zucchini
1/3 cup diced pimento
1/4 cup chopped parsley
Toasted sesame seeds

To prepare the vinaigrette, mince the garlic in a food processor. Add the olive oil, wine vinegar and pepper and process until blended.

To prepare the salad, combine the warm pasta with the olives, celery, zucchini, pimento and parsley in a bowl and toss to mix. Add the vinaigrette and toss to coat. Sprinkle each serving with toasted sesame seeds.

Serves 8 to 10

Colorful Rice Salad with Lemon Dressing

LEMON DRESSING
1/4 cup fresh lemon juice
1/4 cup extra-virgin olive oil
1 teaspoon honey

SALAD
2 green onions, thinly sliced
2 garlic cloves, crushed and minced
1 small summer squash, chopped
1 large tomato, chopped

1 small carrot or radish, grated or minced
1/2 red bell pepper, minced
1 cup spinach leaves, rolled together tightly and thinly sliced
2 tablespoons finely chopped fresh parsley or cilantro
1 1/2 to 2 cups long grain brown rice, cooked
Salt and pepper to taste

To prepare the dressing, place the lemon juice in a small bowl. Add the olive oil in a fine stream, whisking constantly until emulsified. Whisk in the honey.

To prepare the salad, combine the green onions, garlic, squash, tomato, carrot, bell pepper, spinach leaves and parsley in a ceramic or glass bowl and toss to mix. Add the dressing and toss to coat. Cover and chill for 1 hour. Stir in the cooled rice and season with salt and pepper. Chill, covered, until ready to serve. Delicious served with grilled or broiled steak, fish or seafood.

Serves 4

CELERY SEED SALAD DRESSING

Combine 1/2 cup vegetable oil, 1/4 cup vinegar, 2 garlic cloves, minced, 5 tablespoons sugar, 1 teaspoon grated onion, 1 teaspoon salt, 1/2 teaspoon prepared mustard and 1/2 teaspoon celery seeds in a jar with a tight-fitting lid. Seal the jar and shake well. Let stand at room temperature for 3 to 10 hours. Shake vigorously before serving. Makes 1 cup.

HELPFUL HINTS

Soups & Salads

*I*f soup is too salty, add a slice of uncooked potato and boil for a
short time; remove the potato before serving.

Always add salt to the water when cooking meat-stock soups.
Salt will draw out more meat flavor.

To remove grease from soup, place a leaf of lettuce on the hot soup
for a few minutes and remove before serving.

For a healthier alternative, use puréed cooked vegetables to thicken sauces
and soups rather than the more traditional high-fat methods.

Croutons, pastry cutouts, yogurt, or sour cream livens up any soup.
Use crumbled bacon in vegetable soups.

Save the juice from canned tomatoes and freeze in ice cube trays. Store the
cubes in a sealable plastic bag and use for cooking or in tomato drinks.

To add variety to salad dressings, make your favorite oil and vinegar
dressing by the quart. At mealtime, measure the amount you'll need and add
blue cheese, onion, garlic, or a favorite herb.

Perk up soggy lettuce by soaking in a mixture of lemon juice and cold water.

To remove the core from a head of lettuce, hit the core end sharply against
the countertop or side of the sink. Then the core will twist out easily.

Toasted sesame seeds make a great addition to salads.
To toast, sprinkle a thin layer of sesame seeds in a skillet and shake or
stir over low heat until they are a toasty golden brown.

Rubbing waxed paper over the inside and outside of a wooden salad bowl
will prevent it from becoming sticky.

Main Dishes

"*My mother was a good recreational cook, but what she basically believed about cooking was that if you worked hard and prospered, someone else would do it for you.*"

—Nora Ephron

"*There is one thing more exasperating than a wife who can cook and won't, and that's a wife who can't cook and will.*"

—Robert Frost

"*Food, like a loving touch or a glimpse of divine power, has that ability to comfort.*"

—Norman Kolpas

"*One of the nicest things about life is the way we must regularly stop whatever it is we are doing and devote our attention to eating.*"

—Luciano Pavarotti & William Wright

Pamela A Wiebler
2007

Grandmother's Beef Tenderloin

1 (3- to 3^1/2-pound) trimmed
   beef tenderloin
2 tablespoons olive oil
Worcestershire sauce

1 teaspoon garlic powder
1 teaspoon onion powder
1 teaspoon sea salt
^{1}/2 teaspoon freshly ground pepper

Place the tenderloin on a large sheet of foil. Rub the tenderloin with the olive oil and sprinkle with Worcestershire sauce. Mix the garlic powder, onion powder, sea salt and pepper together in a small bowl. Rub over the tenderloin. Place with the foil in a roasting pan and broil for 6 minutes on each side. Wrap in the foil and place in a 400-degree oven. Reduce the oven temperature to 350 degrees. Roast for 20 minutes per pound for medium-rare or to 145 degrees on a meat thermometer, opening the foil during the last 10 minutes of roasting to brown the surface.

Serves 10 to 12

RED WINE MUSHROOM SAUCE

Serve this delicious sauce over sliced beef tenderloin. To prepare the sauce, melt 1 teaspoon butter or margarine in a nonstick skillet over medium heat until bubbly. Add 1 tablespoon minced green onions and ^{1}/2 teaspoon minced garlic and sauté for 2 minutes. Add 3 cups sliced fresh mushrooms and sauté until tender. Stir in ^{1}/2 cup red cooking wine. Bring to a boil and boil for 1 minute. Dissolve 1 teaspoon cornstarch in ^{1}/2 cup beef broth and pour into the mushroom mixture. Bring to a boil and boil for 1 minute, stirring constantly. Season with pepper to taste. Makes 3 cups.

Rosemary Garlic Beef Tenderloin

1/2 cup olive oil
1/2 cup soy sauce
1/4 cup balsamic vinegar or red
    wine vinegar
8 large garlic cloves, minced

4 teaspoons dried
    rosemary, crumbled
1 (4- to 6-pound) beef
    tenderloin, trimmed
Pepper to taste

Combine the olive oil, soy sauce, balsamic vinegar, garlic and rosemary in a glass baking dish. Add the tenderloin, turning to coat. Season well with pepper. Cover and marinate in the refrigerator for 8 to 10 hours, turning occasionally. Remove from the refrigerator and let stand until the tenderloin is room temperature. Place on a grill rack and grill to 145 degrees on a meat thermometer for medium-rare or to 160 degrees for medium. (Note: You may bake the tenderloin in the oven.)

Serves 12 to 15

Barbecued Brisket

1/2 cup soy sauce
2 tablespoons Worcestershire sauce
1 tablespoon dry mustard
1 tablespoon steak sauce
1 tablespoon garlic powder

1 tablespoon liquid smoke
1 teaspoon crushed red pepper
1 (4- to 6-pound) brisket,
    market trimmed
1 (12-ounce) bottle barbecue sauce

Combine the soy sauce, Worcestershire sauce, dry mustard, steak sauce, garlic powder, liquid smoke and red pepper in a bowl and mix well. Place the brisket in a sealable plastic bag and pour the marinade over the brisket. Seal the bag and marinate in the refrigerator for 8 to 10 hours. Place the brisket and marinade in a baking dish. Cover with foil and bake at 300 degrees for 6 hours. Maintain the oven temperature. Drain the brisket, reserving 1 1/2 cups of the marinade. Place the brisket in another baking pan. Combine the reserved marinade and barbecue sauce in a bowl and mix well. Pour the barbecue sauce mixture over the brisket. Bake, covered, for 1 hour longer.

Serves 10 to 12

Filet of Beef with Savory Wild Rice

BEEF

1/2 cup beef or chicken broth
1/4 cup honey
1/4 cup soy sauce
1/2 teaspoon ginger
1/4 teaspoon dry mustard
1/2 garlic clove, crushed
1 to 2 jiggers bourbon or gin
1 (1 1/2-pound) filet of beef, cut
    into 4 steaks

SAVORY WILD RICE

2 tablespoons butter
1 Vidalia onion or other sweet
    onion, chopped
1 cup wild rice, rinsed in
    cold water
2 (14-ounce) cans chicken broth
3 tablespoons almonds, toasted
3 tablespoons raisins
2 tablespoons minced fresh parsley
1/2 teaspoon salt
1/2 teaspoon freshly ground pepper

To prepare the beef, combine the beef broth, honey, soy sauce, ginger, dry mustard and garlic in a small saucepan. Bring to a boil over medium heat and simmer for 5 minutes. Add the bourbon and blend well. Cool for 10 minutes. Place the beef in a nonmetal dish and pour the marinade over the top. Cover and marinate in the refrigerator for 3 to 10 hours, turning the beef at least once. Drain the beef, discarding the marinade. Place the beef on a grill rack coated with nonstick cooking spray. Sear the beef over medium heat for 1 minute on each side. Cover the grill and grill for 4 to 5 minutes on each side or to 145 degrees on a meat thermometer for medium-rare. (To prepare the beef on an indoor grill, place the beef on a preheated grill rack and grill over high heat for 18 to 20 minutes or to 145 degrees on a meat thermometer, turning the beef every 7 minutes.)

To prepare the rice, melt the butter in a medium saucepan over medium heat. Add the onion and sauté for 5 minutes. Spoon the onion into a dish and set aside. Bring the rice and chicken broth to a boil in a saucepan over high heat. Reduce the heat to medium-high and cook for 25 to 30 minutes or until the rice begins to open; drain well. Add the sautéed onion, almonds, raisins, parsley, salt and pepper and mix well. Cover and keep warm at room temperature until ready to serve with the beef. (Note: To toast the almonds, place the almonds in a single layer in a shallow baking pan and bake at 350 degrees for 10 to 15 minutes or until golden brown.)

Serves 4

Stuffed Flank Steak

1 (2- to 2 1/4-pound) untrimmed
    flank steak, or 1 (1 3/4-pound)
    trimmed flank steak
1 cup soy sauce
1 tablespoon meat tenderizer
1 to 2 teaspoons brandy
1 small onion, chopped
1/2 cup chopped green bell pepper
1 cup sliced mushrooms

1 carrot, peeled and chopped
2 garlic cloves, finely chopped
3 tablespoons butter
1 tablespoon chopped fresh cilantro
1/2 teaspoon pepper
2 to 3 tablespoons bread crumbs
2 to 4 slices provolone cheese
Pepper to taste

Pound the steak as thin as possible and place in a sealable plastic bag. Mix the soy sauce, meat tenderizer and brandy in a small bowl. Pour over the steak and seal the bag, turning to coat. Marinate in the refrigerator for 2 hours or longer.

Sauté the onion, bell pepper, mushrooms, carrot and garlic in the butter in a skillet until tender. Add the cilantro and 1/2 teaspoon pepper and mix well. Stir in enough of the bread crumbs to bind the mixture together.

Drain the steak, reserving the marinade. Layer the provolone cheese over the steak and top with the sautéed vegetables. Roll up tightly to enclose the filling and place seam side down in a roasting pan. Pour the reserved marinade over the top and season with pepper to taste. Bake at 350 degrees for 1 hour. Let stand for 5 minutes before slicing to serve.

Serves 4

Stroganoff

2 pounds top round beef,
    cut into strips
1 1/2 cups sliced onions
1/4 cup (1/2 stick) butter
4 garlic cloves, crushed
1/2 cup sherry

1 pound fresh mushrooms,
    sautéed
3 cups sour cream
1 cup tomato soup
Worcestershire sauce to taste
Salt and pepper to taste

Brown the beef with the onions in the butter in a skillet. Add the garlic, sherry, sautéed mushrooms, sour cream, soup, Worcestershire sauce, salt and pepper and mix well. Cook, covered, over low heat for 2 to 4 hours or until tender and cooked through, stirring occasionally. If the mixture is too thin, remove the lid and cook until thickened.

Serves 6

Texas Ribs

BARBECUE SAUCE

2 garlic cloves, minced
1/2 cup chopped onion
2 cups ketchup
3/4 cup chili sauce
2 tablespoons Worcestershire sauce
1 tablespoon soy sauce
2 tablespoons lemon juice
Juice of 1 lime
1/4 cup vinegar
2 tablespoons honey
1 tablespoon brown sugar
Salt and black pepper to taste
Cayenne pepper to taste

RIBS

1/2 cup packed brown sugar
1/4 cup chili powder
1/4 cup cumin
1/4 cup paprika
1 tablespoon lemon pepper
1 tablespoon seasoned salt
1 tablespoon dried garlic
3 pounds beef or pork spare ribs,
    cleaned, trimmed and cut into
    strips between bones

To prepare the sauce, sauté the garlic and onion in a nonstick skillet until brown and tender. Stir in the ketchup and chili sauce. Cook for 3 to 4 minutes, stirring constantly. Stir in the Worcestershire sauce, soy sauce, lemon juice, lime juice, vinegar, honey and brown sugar. Season with the salt, black pepper and cayenne pepper. Reduce the heat to low. Cover and simmer for 30 minutes, adding water if needed for the desired consistency.

To prepare the ribs, mix the brown sugar, chili powder, cumin, paprika, lemon pepper, seasoned salt and garlic in a bowl. Coat the ribs liberally with the rub and place in a 10×15-inch baking pan. Cover and chill for at least 8 hours. Pour the sauce over the ribs. Bake, covered, at 325 degrees for 1 1/2 hours or until tender. Remove the ribs from the sauce and place on a rack in a baking pan. Cool the sauce enough to skim off the fat. Increase the oven temperature to 450 degrees. Bake the ribs for 20 minutes or until brown, turning occasionally and basting with the sauce during the last 10 minutes of baking. (Note: The ribs may be grilled for 20 minutes.)

Serves 6

Salsa Cheeseburgers

1 egg
1/3 cup salsa
1/2 teaspoon cumin
1/2 teaspoon grainy-textured kosher salt
1/4 teaspoon cayenne pepper
1/4 teaspoon freshly ground black pepper
1/4 cup dry fine Italian bread crumbs
1 pound lean ground beef
1/2 cup (2 ounces) shredded Cheddar cheese or
   your favorite cheese

Whisk the egg, salsa, cumin, kosher salt, cayenne pepper and black pepper in a bowl until blended. Stir in the bread crumbs. Add the ground beef and mix together using a fork or your hands. Add the Cheddar cheese and mix until just blended. (Overmixing will toughen the ground beef.) Shape the mixture into 4 patties about 3/4 inch thick. Place on an oiled grill rack and grill, covered, for 6 to 8 minutes per side or until cooked through. Serve on your favorite crusty buns with a spicy salsa or guacamole.

Serves 4

SWEET DILL SLICES

Drain about four-fifths of the liquid from one 16-ounce jar of hamburger dill pickle slices. Remove and reserve about one-half of the pickles. Place 2 garlic cloves and 1/4 teaspoon red pepper flakes in the jar with the remaining pickles. Return the reserved pickles to the jar and add 2 garlic cloves and 1/4 teaspoon red pepper flakes. Fill the jar with sugar. Wipe the mouth of the jar well and tighten the lid. Store in the refrigerator, inverting the jar and shaking slightly every few hours for the first couple of days. The pickles are ready to serve when the sugar is dissolved. Makes 16 ounces.

Beef and Pork Green Chili

$1/4$ cup ($1/2$ stick) unsalted butter
$1/4$ cup all-purpose flour
8 ounces ground beef
8 ounces ground pork
8 ounces lean stew beef
1 tablespoon vegetable oil
1 large onion, chopped
3 garlic cloves, minced
3 tablespoons unsalted butter
$1/3$ cup chopped coriander

1 tablespoon minced parsley
2 teaspoons Tabasco sauce
1 teaspoon dried crumbled oregano
2 teaspoons cumin
$1/2$ teaspoon pepper
2 tablespoons all-purpose flour
3 to 5 cups beef broth
2 pounds canned chopped
   green chiles

To prepare a roux, melt $1/4$ cup butter in a small skillet. Stir in $1/4$ cup flour and cook for 3 minutes, stirring constantly. Brown the ground beef, ground pork and stew beef in batches in the hot oil in a large stockpot until cooked through, stirring constantly. Remove the beef mixture with a slotted spoon and place in a bowl. Cook the onion, garlic and 3 tablespoons butter in the pan drippings until softened. Add the coriander, parsley, Tabasco sauce, oregano, cumin, pepper and 2 tablespoons flour. Cook for 2 to 3 minutes or until the flour is brown. Add the beef broth and green chiles and mix well. Return the beef mixture to the stockpot. Add the roux and stir until incorporated. Simmer for 1 hour. Remove from the heat and let stand to cool completely. Chill, covered, for 8 to 10 hours. Reheat to serve. Ladle into serving bowls and serve with corn chips, shredded sharp Cheddar cheese and sour cream.

Makes 10 cups

Green Enchiladas

GREEN CHILE SAUCE

1 (12-ounce) can evaporated milk
8 ounces Velveeta cheese, cubed
3 tablespoons all-purpose flour
1/4 cup (1/2 stick) butter
1 (4-ounce) can green chiles
1 (2-ounce) jar pimento

ENCHILADAS

1 1/2 pounds ground beef
10 (6- to 7-inch) flour tortillas
1 tablespoon vegetable oil
1 onion, chopped
8 ounces Cheddar cheese, shredded

To prepare the sauce, combine the evaporated milk, Velveeta cheese, flour, butter, green chiles and pimento in a saucepan. Cook over low heat until the cheese is melted, stirring frequently.

To prepare the enchiladas, brown the ground beef in a skillet, stirring until crumbly; drain. Brown the tortillas lightly one at a time in the oil in a skillet, turning once. Fill each tortilla with the ground beef, onion and Cheddar cheese and roll up to enclose the filling. Place in a 9×13-inch glass baking dish. Pour the sauce over the top. Bake at 325 degrees for 20 minutes.

Serves 6

Slow-Cooker Enchiladas

1 pound ground beef
1/4 to 1/2 cup chopped onion
1 envelope taco seasoning mix
Salt and pepper to taste
2 (15-ounce) cans chili with beans
2 (10-ounce) cans fiesta nacho
  cheese soup

2 (10-ounce) cans cream of
  chicken soup
1/2 to 1 cup water
1 (8-ounce) can tomato sauce
1 (4-ounce) can diced green chiles
18 corn tortillas
2 cups (8 ounces) shredded
  Cheddar cheese

Brown the ground beef in a skillet, stirring until crumbly; drain. Stir in the onion, taco seasoning mix, salt and pepper. Combine the chili with beans, nacho cheese soup and chicken soup in a heated slow cooker and mix well. Stir in the water and tomato sauce. Add the green chiles and ground beef mixture and mix well. Cook on High for at least 2 hours. Cut the tortillas into quarters and poke one at a time into the hot ground beef mixture to prevent clumping together. Sprinkle with the Cheddar cheese or stir the cheese into the mixture. Cook on High for 30 minutes and serve. (Note: You may use cream of mushroom soup or cream of onion soup instead of the cream of chicken soup.)

Serves 8

Lamb Shish Kabobs

2 pounds tender lamb, boned and cut into cubes
Juice of 2 large lemons
1/4 cup olive oil
2 tablespoons grated onion
1 garlic clove
1 tablespoon chopped jalapeño chile
1 tablespoon pepper juice
1 teaspoon coriander
1 teaspoon ginger
2 teaspoons curry powder
1 tablespoon salt
1 large onion, cut into quarters and separated
1 large green bell pepper, cut into quarters and halved
16 to 18 mushrooms
4 small tomatoes, cut into quarters

Place the lamb in a sealable plastic bag. Mix the lemon juice, olive oil, grated onion, garlic, jalapeño chile, pepper juice, coriander, ginger, curry powder and salt in a bowl. Pour over the lamb and seal the bag. Marinate in the refrigerator for 2 hours.

Blanch the pieces of onion and bell pepper by plunging into boiling water in a saucepan and then immediately plunging into cold water to stop the cooking process; drain.

Drain the lamb, reserving the marinade. Thread the lamb alternately with the onion, bell pepper, mushrooms and tomatoes onto six 12-inch-long skewers. Place on a rack in a broiler pan. Broil for 8 minutes on each side, basting with the reserved marinade.

Serves 6

Slow-Cooker Pork Tenderloin

1 (16-ounce) can whole
　　cranberry sauce
1/2 cup sugar
2 teaspoons vinegar
1 teaspoon dry mustard
1 teaspoon salt

1/4 to 1/2 teaspoon crushed
　　red pepper
1 onion, chopped
1/2 cup coarsely chopped apricots
6 ounces apricot nectar
1 (2 1/2-pound) boneless pork
　　loin roast, well trimmed

Combine the cranberry sauce, sugar, vinegar, dry mustard, salt and red pepper
in a bowl and stir to mix. Reserve a small amount of the onion and apricots
for garnish. Stir the remaining onion and apricots into the cranberry mixture.
Add the apricot nectar and mix well. Place the pork in a slow cooker. Pour the
cranberry mixture over the pork to cover. Cook on Low for at least 5 hours or
until the pork is cooked through. Cut the pork into 1/2-inch slices and serve
with the sauce. Garnish with the reserved onion and apricots. (Note: If a thicker
sauce is desired, thicken with 1 teaspoon cornstarch.)

Serves 6

COCA-COLA HABANERO BARBECUE SAUCE

*Chop 3 or 4 fresh jalapeño chiles and 3 or 4 habanero chiles while
wearing rubber gloves and place in a large nonmetal bowl. Add 2 cups
Coca-Cola and let stand for 4 hours at room temperature. (This will take the
"bite" out of the chiles while leaving the flavor.) Add 1 gallon of barbecue sauce,
1/4 cup sugar, Tony Chachere's seasoning to taste and pepper to taste and mix well.*
　　　　　　　　　　　　　　　　　　　　　　Makes 1 gallon.

Braised Pork Loin

1 (3- to 4-pound) pork loin
Salt and pepper to taste
24 ounces dark beer

1 cup dried cherries
3 or 4 garlic cloves, sliced

Cut the pork into slices 1 inch thick. Season each slice with salt and pepper. Sear the pork in a very hot 5-quart sauté pan for 4 minutes per side or until golden brown. Reduce the heat and add the beer, cherries and garlic. Cover and cook over low heat until the pork is cooked through and tender. (Note: To finish this dish in a slow cooker, remove the pork after browning to a slow cooker. Add half the beer to the hot sauté pan, stirring to deglaze the pan. Add with the remaining ingredients to the pork. Cook on Low for 8 hours or cook on High for 2 to 3 hours.)

Serves 6 to 8

Grilled Marinated Pork Chops

1 cup soy sauce
1/4 cup vegetable oil
1/4 cup honey

1 1/4 teaspoons ginger
2 garlic cloves, minced
8 thick pork chops

Combine the soy sauce, oil, honey, ginger and garlic in a small saucepan and mix well. Heat over low heat to combine, stirring frequently. Remove from the heat to cool. Place the pork chops in a sealable plastic bag. Pour the sauce over the pork chops and seal the bag. Marinate in the refrigerator for 4 to 10 hours, turning frequently. Drain the pork chops, reserving the marinade. Place the pork chops on a grill rack. Grill over medium heat until the pork chops are cooked through, basting with the reserved marinade.

Serves 8

THREE-PEPPER CHUTNEY

Chop 3 red bell peppers, 3 green bell peppers and 1 onion and place in a saucepan. Remove the seeds from 3 jalapeño chiles and mince the chiles. Add the jalapeño chiles, 1 1/2 cups packed brown sugar, 1 1/2 cups apple cider vinegar and 1 teaspoon salt to the saucepan. Bring to a boil and reduce the heat. Simmer for 1 to 2 hours or until syrupy. Spoon into a bowl. Chill, covered, in the refrigerator before serving. Makes 4 cups.

Pancetta Carbonara

1 tablespoon butter
4 slices bacon, chopped
4 slices pancetta, chopped
1/4 teaspoon ground cinnamon
2 cups whipping cream
3/4 cup (3 ounces) freshly grated
   Parmesan cheese

3/4 cup (3 ounces) freshly
   grated Romano cheese
6 egg yolks
18 ounces fresh fettuccini
Salt and freshly ground pepper
   to taste
2 tablespoons chopped fresh chives

Melt the butter in a large skillet over medium heat. Add the bacon and pancetta and cook for 5 minutes or until crisp and light brown. Sprinkle with the cinnamon and sauté for 2 minutes longer or until the bacon is crisp and golden. Remove from the heat to cool. Whisk in the whipping cream, Parmesan cheese, Romano cheese and egg yolks.

Cook the pasta in boiling salted water in a large saucepan over high heat for 3 minutes or until tender but still firm to the bite, stirring occasionally; drain. Add the hot pasta to the cream mixture. Cook for 5 minutes over medium-low heat until the sauce thickly coats the pasta, tossing constantly. Do not boil. Season with salt and pepper. Place in a large wide serving bowl and sprinkle with the chives.

Serves 6

Tortellini Alfredo

2 (9-ounce) packages refrigerated
   cheese-filled tortellini
1 cup whipping cream
3/4 cup (3 ounces) freshly grated
   Parmesan cheese

3 slices prosciutto, chopped
3 marinated artichoke hearts, sliced
Freshly ground pepper to taste

Prepare the tortellini using the package directions; drain. Heat the whipping cream in a large skillet over low heat. Gradually sprinkle in 1/2 cup of the Parmesan cheese, stirring constantly until blended after each addition. Simmer for 15 to 20 minutes, stirring occasionally. Add the tortellini, prosciutto and artichoke hearts. Simmer for 5 to 10 minutes or until the sauce is slightly reduced, stirring occasionally. Place on individual serving plates and top evenly with the remaining 1/4 cup Parmesan cheese and freshly ground pepper. Serve immediately.

Serves 4 to 6

Ham-Stuffed Manicotti

SWISS CHEESE SAUCE

1/4 cup chopped green bell pepper
3 tablespoons butter
3 tablespoons all-purpose flour
2 cups milk
1 cup (4 ounces) shredded
   Swiss cheese

MANICOTTI

8 manicotti
1/2 teaspoon salt
1/4 cup chopped onion
2 tablespoons vegetable oil
3 cups ground cooked ham
1 cup chopped mushrooms
3 tablespoons grated
   Parmesan cheese

To prepare the sauce, sauté the bell pepper in the butter in a small saucepan until tender. Add the flour and cook for 3 minutes, stirring constantly. Add the milk and cook until thickened, stirring constantly. Remove from the heat. Add the Swiss cheese and stir until melted.

To prepare the manicotti, cook the manicotti in boiling salted water in a large saucepan until tender but still firm. Rinse with cold water and drain well. Sauté the onion in the oil in a skillet until tender. Add the ham, mushrooms and Parmesan cheese and mix well. Stuff the manicotti with the ham mixture and place in a 9×13-inch shallow baking dish. Cover with the cheese sauce. Bake at 350 degrees for 30 minutes or until hot and bubbly.

Serves 4

PINEAPPLE SAUCE

Mix 2 cups packed brown sugar and 2 tablespoons cornstarch in a saucepan. Stir in one 20-ounce can crushed pineapple, 2 tablespoons prepared mustard and 1 1/2 tablespoons lemon juice. Bring to a boil and boil for 1 minute, stirring constantly. Serve as a sauce or use as a glaze for ham. Serves 15.

Chicken with Green Chile–Peach Sauce

1 (21-ounce) can peach pie filling
1 (14-ounce) can chicken broth
2 (2¹/2- to 3-pound) whole
* chickens, quartered*
Olive oil
¹/2 teaspoon each salt and pepper

1 (4-ounce) can chopped
* green chiles*
1 garlic clove, minced
¹/2 cup chopped onion
2 tablespoons chopped fresh cilantro
* or parsley*

Process one-half of the peach filling and one-half of the chicken broth in a blender or food processor until smooth. Place the chicken in a large roasting pan and coat with olive oil. Season with the salt and pepper. Brush with the peach mixture. Bake at 350 degrees for 1 hour or until cooked through. Process the remaining peach filling and the green chiles in a blender or food processor until smooth. Sauté the garlic and onion in a skillet for 2 minutes or until tender. Add the remaining chicken broth and cook for 3 to 5 minutes. Add the green chile mixture and cook until heated through. Stir in the cilantro. Serve over the chicken.

Serves 6 to 8

Apricot Pecan Chicken

2/3 cup sherry or white wine
¹/2 cup chicken stock
12 ounces dried apricots
4 boneless chicken breasts
3 tablespoons olive oil
2 tablespoons butter
¹/2 teaspoon salt

¹/4 teaspoon pepper
1 cup chicken stock
1 tablespoon finely chopped shallots
1 tablespoon tomato paste
2 tablespoons grainy mustard
¹/2 cup pecans, toasted and chopped
1 scallion, thinly sliced

Bring the wine and ¹/2 cup chicken stock to a boil in a small saucepan. Turn off the heat and add the apricots. Steep for 30 minutes or until the apricots are soft. Sauté the chicken in the hot olive oil and butter in a heavy skillet over medium heat until light and golden on both sides. Sprinkle with the salt and pepper. Drain the apricots, reserving the liquid. Add the apricot liquid and 1 cup chicken stock to the chicken. Reduce the heat to low and cook for 5 to 8 minutes or until the chicken is cooked through. Remove the chicken to a plate and keep warm. Add the apricots and shallots to the skillet and simmer for 2 minutes. Add the tomato paste and mustard. Simmer for 3 minutes, stirring constantly. Return the chicken to the skillet. Cook for 1 to 2 minutes or until heated through. Place the chicken and apricots on a serving platter. Sprinkle with the pecans and scallion.

Serves 4

Chicken with Artichokes and Tomatoes

1 1/4 pounds boneless chicken breasts	2 garlic cloves, sliced
1/2 teaspoon salt	1 (14-ounce) can stewed tomatoes
1/2 teaspoon oregano	1 (9-ounce) package frozen
1/4 teaspoon pepper	artichoke hearts
1 tablespoon olive oil	1 tablespoon capers, rinsed
1 small onion, chopped	and drained

Trim the chicken and pound thin. Mix the salt, oregano and pepper together and rub over the chicken. Cook the chicken in the hot olive oil in a large skillet over medium heat for 2 minutes per side or until golden and cooked through. Remove the chicken from the skillet and keep warm. Increase the heat to medium-high and add the onion to the skillet. Cook for 2 minutes. Add the garlic and cook for 30 seconds, stirring constantly. Stir in the undrained tomatoes. Cook for 3 minutes. Reduce the heat to medium and return the chicken to the skillet. Add the artichoke hearts and capers and mix gently. Cook for 3 to 5 minutes or until heated through.

Serves 4

Chicken Artichoke Casserole

4 chicken breasts	1 (10-ounce) can cream of
2 (14-ounce) cans artichoke	celery soup
hearts, drained and chopped	8 ounces Velveeta cheese
1 (10-ounce) can cream of	1/2 cup mayonnaise
chicken soup	3 tablespoons fresh lemon juice
	1/2 cup sour cream

Boil the chicken breasts in water to cover in a saucepan for 1 1/2 hours. Drain the chicken, discarding the skin and bones. Chop the chicken into bite-size pieces. Layer the artichoke hearts and chicken evenly in a 3-quart baking dish. Combine the chicken soup, celery soup, Velveeta cheese, mayonnaise and lemon juice in a double boiler. Cook over hot water until the Velveeta cheese melts, stirring frequently. Remove from the heat and stir in the sour cream. Pour over the layers. Bake at 350 degrees for 35 minutes.

Serves 8

Brie-Stuffed Chicken Breasts

2 tablespoons olive oil
1 onion, chopped
1 Granny Smith apple, cored and
   coarsely chopped
$1/2$ teaspoon dried thyme
$1/2$ teaspoon salt
$1/4$ teaspoon pepper
$1/4$ cup apple cider vinegar
4 ounces Brie cheese, rind removed and
   cheese cut into chunks
4 chicken breasts
$1/2$ teaspoon dried thyme
$1/2$ teaspoon salt
$1/4$ teaspoon pepper
$1/2$ cup apple cider vinegar

Heat the olive oil in a medium saucepan over medium heat. Add the onion and sauté until tender. Add the apple, $1/2$ teaspoon thyme, $1/2$ teaspoon salt, $1/4$ teaspoon pepper and $1/4$ cup apple cider vinegar. Cook until the apple is tender. Remove from the heat and cool slightly. Stir in the Brie cheese and divide the stuffing into 4 equal portions.

Run your fingers under the skin of the chicken to separate. Place the stuffing under the skin of each chicken breast. Place in a 9×13-inch baking dish. Bake at 400 degrees for 35 minutes or to 170 degrees on a meat thermometer. Remove the chicken to a platter and keep warm.

Skim the fat from the baking dish. Place the drippings in a saucepan, scraping up all the brown bits. Add $1/2$ teaspoon thyme, $1/2$ teaspoon salt, $1/4$ teaspoon pepper and $1/2$ cup apple cider vinegar. Cook over medium heat until the mixture is reduced by one-half. Spoon over the chicken and serve.

Serves 4

Southwest White Chili

SPICE BLEND
1 teaspoon garlic powder
1 teaspoon cumin
1/2 teaspoon oregano leaves
1/2 teaspoon dried cilantro
1/4 teaspoon red pepper

CHILI
1 pound boneless skinless chicken
   breasts, cut into cubes

1 tablespoon olive oil
1/4 cup chopped yellow onion
1 cup chicken stock or broth
1 (4-ounce) can chopped green chiles
1 (19-ounce) can Great
   Northern beans
1 cup (4 ounces) shredded
   Monterey Jack cheese

To prepare the spice blend, mix the garlic powder, cumin, oregano, cilantro and red pepper in a small bowl.

To prepare the chili, cook the chicken in the hot olive oil in a 2- to 3-quart saucepan over medium-high heat for 4 to 5 minutes or until cooked through, stirring frequently. Remove the chicken with a slotted spoon to a bowl, reserving the drippings in the saucepan. Sauté the onion in the reserved drippings for 3 to 4 minutes or until tender. Stir in the chicken stock, green chiles and spice blend. Simmer over low heat for 30 minutes. Return the chicken to the saucepan. Stir in the undrained beans. Simmer for 10 minutes. Ladle into bowls and top with the Monterey Jack cheese.

Serves 4

Salsa Verde Chicken Enchiladas

1 small package white corn
   tortillas, cut into quarters
4 chicken breasts, cooked
   and chopped
3 (7-ounce) cans salsa verde

2 cups (8 ounces) shredded
   Monterey Jack cheese
1 pint heavy whipping
   cream, whipped

Layer the tortilla quarters, chicken, salsa verde, Monterey Jack cheese and whipped cream one-half at a time in a greased 9×13-inch baking pan. Cover and bake for 35 minutes. Uncover and bake for 5 to 10 minutes longer or until light brown. Let stand for 5 minutes before serving.

Serves 6 to 8

Lemon Chicken with Lemon Rice

LEMON RICE
$1/2$ cup uncooked rice
Salt to taste
2 cups water
Grated lemon zest to taste
Chopped parsley to taste
1 tablespoon butter

CHICKEN
1 (1-pound) package chicken tenders
Juice of 1 lemon, or $1/4$ cup thawed
    frozen lemon juice
Seasoned all-purpose flour
$1/2$ cup (1 stick) butter, melted
2 tablespoons chopped parsley
Grated zest of 1 lemon

To prepare the rice, cook the rice in boiling salted water in a saucepan until the water is absorbed. Remove from the heat and stir in lemon zest, parsley and butter.

To prepare the chicken, dip the chicken in the lemon juice and dredge lightly in the flour. Sauté in the butter in a skillet over medium heat for 4 minutes per side, turning once. Mix a small amount of water with the remaining lemon juice and pour carefully around the chicken. Sprinkle with the parsley and lemon zest. Cover and simmer until ready to serve. Serve over the rice.

Serves 4

Grilled Lime Chicken

4 boneless skinless chicken breasts
1/4 cup lime juice
2 tablespoons vegetable oil
1/2 teaspoon ground red pepper
6 garlic cloves, minced
1/2 cup finely chopped red
   bell pepper
1 tablespoon purple onion

1 cup canned black beans,
   drained and rinsed
1 garlic clove
1/2 cup orange juice
2 tablespoons balsamic vinegar
1/4 teaspoon salt
1/8 teaspoon black pepper

Place the chicken in a sealable plastic bag. Combine the lime juice, oil, red pepper and minced garlic in a bowl. Pour one-half of the marinade over the chicken and seal the bag. Store the remaining marinade in the refrigerator. Marinate the chicken in the refrigerator for 1 hour.

Place the bell pepper and onion on a microwave-safe plate and cover with waxed paper. Microwave on High for 1 minute. Process the black beans, garlic clove, orange juice, balsamic vinegar, salt and black pepper in a food processor until smooth. Pour into a saucepan and cook over medium heat until heated through. Keep warm.

Drain the chicken, discarding the marinade. Place the chicken on a grill rack and grill over medium coals for 5 minutes per side or until cooked through, basting with the reserved marinade. Place the chicken on a serving plate and pour the warm bean sauce over the top. Garnish with the bell pepper and onion.

Serves 4

Slow-Cooker Swiss Chicken

4 to 6 boneless chicken breasts
6 to 8 slices Swiss cheese
1 (10-ounce) can cream of
   chicken soup

1/4 cup milk
2 cups dry stuffing mix
1/2 cup (1 stick) butter,
   melted

Place the chicken in a slow cooker sprayed with nonstick cooking spray. Place the Swiss cheese on top of the chicken. Blend the soup and milk in a bowl and pour over the cheese. Layer the stuffing mix over the top and drizzle with the butter. Cover and cook on Low for 8 hours or on High for 6 hours.

Serves 4 to 6

Chicken Sateh

CHICKEN

2 pounds chicken breasts
1 cup soy sauce
3 garlic cloves, minced
1 teaspoon salt
1 teaspoon pepper
Vegetable oil

SATEH SAUCE

1/2 cup (4 ounces) peanut butter
1 cup hot water
1 teaspoon crushed red chiles
1/4 cup molasses
2 tablespoons soy sauce
1 garlic clove, minced
Few drops of lemon juice

To prepare the chicken, cut the chicken into bite-size pieces and place in a sealable plastic bag. Mix the soy sauce, garlic, salt and pepper in a bowl. Pour over the chicken and seal the bag. Marinate in the refrigerator for 1 to 10 hours. Drain the chicken, discarding the marinade. Thread the chicken onto skewers and baste with oil. Place on a rack in a broiler pan. Bake at 325 degrees until the chicken is cooked through, turning frequently.

To prepare the sauce, mix the peanut butter with the water in a saucepan. Stir in the red chiles, molasses, soy sauce, garlic and lemon juice. Simmer for 5 minutes. Serve with the chicken. (Note: The chicken may be grilled.)

Serves 8

PEACH SAUCE

Combine one 6-ounce jar peach baby food, 1/2 cup packed brown sugar, 1/3 cup ketchup, 1/3 cup white vinegar, 2 tablespoons soy sauce, 1 teaspoon ginger and 2 garlic cloves, minced, in a bowl and mix well. Spoon into a jar with a tight-fitting lid. Seal the jar and chill in the refrigerator for up to 2 weeks. Makes 1 1/2 cups.

Tandoori Chicken

GARAM MASALA

1 teaspoon cumin
1 teaspoon coriander
1 teaspoon pepper
Pinch of ground cinnamon
Pinch of ground cloves

CHICKEN

3 pounds chicken pieces
Juice of 1 lemon
1/2 cup plain yogurt
1 to 2 garlic cloves, minced
1/2 teaspoon chili powder
Salt to taste
Sliced limes
Sliced onions
Chopped cilantro

To prepare the garam masala, combine the cumin, coriander, pepper, cinnamon and cloves in a small bowl and mix well. (Note: Prepare the garam masala in bulk and store in a sealable freezer bag in the freezer. Use 1 tablespoon of the mixture in this recipe.)

To prepare the chicken, remove the skin from the chicken and pierce the chicken with a fork. Place in a baking dish and drizzle with the lemon juice. Combine the garam masala, yogurt, garlic, chili powder and salt in a bowl and mix well. Coat the chicken with the yogurt mixture and return to the baking dish. Cover and marinate in the refrigerator for 3 to 10 hours. Bake, covered, at 350 degrees for 50 to 60 minutes or until cooked through. Uncover and broil for 5 to 10 minutes or until brown. Garnish with sliced limes, sliced onions and cilantro.

Serves 6 to 8

Hawaiian Teriyaki Chicken

1 cup soy sauce
1/3 cup dry sherry
1 tablespoon vegetable oil
1/2 cup packed brown sugar
1 tablespoon minced garlic
2 tablespoons grated fresh ginger or
   grated ginger in a jar

3 green onions, cut into
   1-inch lengths
2 pounds chicken breasts or thighs
1 tablespoon cornstarch
2 tablespoons water

Combine the soy sauce, sherry, oil, brown sugar, garlic, ginger and green onions in a medium microwave-safe bowl and mix well. Microwave on High for 2 to 3 minutes or until the mixture boils to blend the flavors. Let stand until cool.

Pat the chicken dry with paper towels and place in sealable plastic bags. Pour the cooled marinade over the chicken and seal the bags. Marinate in the refrigerator for 3 to 10 hours. Place the undrained chicken in a large saucepan and bring to a boil. Simmer for 20 to 25 minutes to ensure the flavor stays in the chicken and to partially cook the chicken. Drain the chicken, reserving the marinade. Place the chicken on a grill rack. Grill for 10 to 15 minutes or until the chicken is cooked through, basting frequently with the reserved marinade. Cool the chicken slightly.

Bring the remaining marinade to a boil in a saucepan. Stir in the cornstarch and water. Cook until thickened, stirring constantly. Serve with the chicken. (Note: The chicken may be baked in a 350-degree oven for 30 to 45 minutes or until cooked through.)

Serves 6

PEPPER RUB

Combine 4 1/2 teaspoons garlic powder, 1 tablespoon dried thyme, 2 teaspoons freshly ground black pepper, 1 1/2 teaspoons salt, 1 1/2 teaspoons lemon pepper, 1 1/2 teaspoons chopped fresh parsley and 1 1/2 teaspoons ground red pepper in a bowl and mix well. To use, brush steak, chicken or pork with 3 tablespoons olive oil and rub with the seasoning mixture. Chill for 1 hour before grilling.

Bow Tie Pasta with Chicken and Asiago Sun-Dried Tomato Sauce

ASIAGO SUN-DRIED TOMATO SAUCE

2 cups heavy cream
1 chicken bouillon cube
1 tablespoon asiago cheese
1 tablespoon cornstarch
1 tablespoon water
1 cup chopped sun-dried tomatoes

PASTA

16 ounces bow tie pasta
Salt to taste

1/4 cup (1/2 stick) butter
1 cup diced red onion
2 garlic cloves, chopped
1 cup crumbled cooked bacon
1 cup chopped green onions
1 pound grilled boneless skinless
   chicken breasts, chopped
1 cup heavy cream
2 tablespoons chopped fresh parsley
2 tablespoons grated Romano cheese
Freshly ground pepper to taste

To prepare the sauce, heat the cream in a large saucepan over medium heat until just bubbling. Add the bouillon cube and asiago cheese and whisk until the bouillon cube is dissolved. Dissolve the cornstarch in the water and stir into the sauce. Cook until thickened, stirring constantly. Stir in the sun-dried tomatoes and set aside. (You may cover and chill in the refrigerator until ready to use.)

To prepare the pasta, cook the pasta in boiling salted water in a large stockpot for 8 to 10 minutes or until al dente; drain. Melt the butter in a large saucepan over medium heat. Add the onion and sauté until tender and translucent. Stir in the garlic and bacon and cook for 2 minutes. Stir in the green onions, chicken and cream. Cook until the cream is heated through, stirring constantly. Add the sauce and cook until heated through. Pour over the pasta and toss until evenly coated. Place in a large serving bowl and sprinkle with the chopped parsley, Romano cheese and pepper.

Serves 6

Savory Crescent Chicken Squares

3 ounces cream cheese, softened
2 tablespoons butter, softened
2 cups cubed cooked chicken
1 tablespoon chopped onion
1/4 cup chopped mushrooms
2 tablespoons milk
1 tablespoon drained chopped
  pimento (optional)

1/4 teaspoon salt
1/8 teaspoon pepper
1 (8-count) can refrigerator
  crescent rolls
1 tablespoon butter, melted
3/4 cup crushed seasoned crackers

Beat the cream cheese and 2 tablespoons butter in a medium bowl until smooth. Add the chicken, onion, mushrooms, milk, pimento, salt and pepper and mix well. Separate the roll dough into four rectangles, pressing the perforations to seal. Spoon 1/2 cup of the chicken mixture in the center of each rectangle. Pull the four corners of the dough to the center of the chicken mixture and twist firmly, pinching the edges to seal. Place on an ungreased baking sheet and brush the tops with the melted butter. Sprinkle with the crackers. Bake at 350 degrees for 25 to 30 minutes or until golden brown.

Serves 4 to 8

Cajun Fried Turkey

1 (16-ounce) bottle Italian
  salad dressing
1 (4-ounce) bottle Louisiana
  hot sauce
1/4 cup Cajun seasoning

1 tablespoon garlic powder
Water
1 (10- to 17-pound) frozen
  turkey, thawed
Peanut oil for frying

Strain the salad dressing into a bowl. Add the hot sauce, Cajun seasoning, garlic powder and enough water to measure 1 quart. Use a syringe to inject the mixture into the thawed turkey. Chill in the refrigerator for 8 to 10 hours.

Heat enough peanut oil to cover the turkey to 350 degrees in a large deep fryer or 24-quart stockpot. (This usually takes about 45 minutes.) Lower the turkey into the hot oil and cook for 3 1/2 minutes per pound or until a meat thermometer registers 170 degrees when inserted in the breast and 180 degrees when inserted in the thigh.

Serves 12 to 24

Duck Deluxe

3 cups water
2 chicken bouillon cubes
Garlic salt to taste
1 teaspoon salt
Dash of pepper
2 tablespoons Worcestershire sauce
3/4 to 1 cup half-and-half
1/2 cup sherry
2 wild ducks

Bacon drippings or margarine
Chopped apple to taste
Chopped onion to taste
Chopped celery to taste
3 to 4 tablespoons
    all-purpose flour
Juice of 2 oranges
1/4 cup orange marmalade
1/2 cup brandy

Pour the water into a large skillet, adding additional water if needed to fill the skillet one-half full. Heat the water until hot. Dissolve the bouillon cubes in the hot water and sprinkle generously with garlic salt. Add the salt, pepper, Worcestershire sauce, half-and-half and wine. Heat just until the mixture begins to boil but do not boil.

Brown the ducks on all sides in bacon drippings in a large seasoned cast-iron skillet or Dutch oven. Stuff the ducks with apple, onion and celery and place breast side down in the skillet. Pour the liquid mixture over the ducks. Cover tightly and bake at 350 degrees for 2 to 2 1/2 hours, basting or turning the ducks in the liquid every 30 minutes. Remove the ducks from the liquid. Stir the flour gradually into the liquid in the skillet. Add the orange juice, marmalade and brandy. Cook until thickened, stirring constantly. Slice the ducks and place in the gravy in the skillet. Cook until heated through and serve.

Serves 8

Seafood Paella

1 tablespoon sweet paprika
2 teaspoons dried oregano
Kosher salt and freshly ground
    pepper to taste
1 (3-pound) chicken, cut into
    10 pieces
3 (3-ounce) chorizos, cut into
    small pieces
2 tablespoons extra-virgin olive oil
Kosher salt and freshly ground
    pepper to taste
2 tablespoons extra-virgin olive oil
1 red onion, chopped
4 garlic cloves, chopped
2 tablespoons finely chopped fresh
    flat-leaf parsley

1 (15-ounce) can whole tomatoes,
    drained and hand crushed
1 teaspoon paprika
1 green bell pepper, chopped
1 red bell pepper, chopped
1 tablespoon extra-virgin olive oil
4 cups short grain Spanish rice
6 cups warm water
Pinch of saffron threads
12 littleneck clams, scrubbed
1 pound jumbo shrimp, peeled
    and deveined
2 lobster tails
1/2 cup thawed frozen green peas
Chopped flat-leaf parsley
Lemon wedges

Mix 1 tablespoon paprika, the oregano, kosher salt and pepper in a small bowl. Rub the spice mixture over the chicken. Place the chicken in a sealable plastic bag and seal. Marinate in the refrigerator for 1 hour.

Sauté the sausages in 2 tablespoons hot olive oil in a wide shallow skillet over medium-high heat until brown. Remove the sausages from the skillet and keep warm. Place the chicken skin side down in the skillet. Brown the chicken on all sides, turning with tongs. Season with kosher salt and freshly ground pepper. Remove the chicken from the skillet and keep warm.

To prepare a sofrito, spoon 2 tablespoons olive oil into the skillet. Add the onion, garlic and 2 tablespoons parsley and sauté for 2 to 3 minutes over medium heat. Add the tomatoes and 1 teaspoon paprika and cook until all the liquid from the tomatoes evaporates. Spoon the sofrito into a bowl and wipe the skillet clean.

Sauté the bell peppers in 1 tablespoon olive oil in a skillet for 6 minutes. Add the sofrito to the skillet. Fold in the rice and stir-fry to coat the grains. Add the water and simmer for 10 minutes, gently moving the skillet around so the rice cooks evenly and absorbs the liquid. Add the chicken, sausages and saffron. Tuck the clams and shrimp into the rice mixture. Cook for 8 minutes or until the shrimp turns pink. Simmer for 15 minutes or until the rice is al dente; do not stir. During the last 5 minutes of cooking, add the lobster tails and peas. Cover the pan with foil and let rest for 5 minutes. Garnish with additional parsley and lemon wedges.

Serves 4 to 6

Skillet-Grilled Catfish

1/4 cup all-purpose flour
1/4 cup cornmeal
1 teaspoon onion powder
1 teaspoon dried basil
1/2 teaspoon garlic salt
1/2 teaspoon dried thyme

1/2 teaspoon white pepper
1/2 teaspoon cayenne pepper
1/2 teaspoon black pepper
4 (6- to 8-ounce) catfish fillets
1/4 cup (1/2 stick) butter

Mix the flour, cornmeal, onion powder, basil, garlic salt, thyme, white pepper, cayenne pepper and black pepper in a large sealable plastic bag. Add the fish one at a time and shake to coat. Melt the butter in a large cast-iron skillet on a grill rack over medium heat. Add the catfish and grill, covered, for 4 minutes on each side or until the fish flakes easily with a fork.

Serves 4

Fillet of Sole Véronique

6 small fillets of sole
    (about 1 1/2 pounds)
1 teaspoon salt
White pepper to taste
3 tablespoons butter
1 1/2 cups dry white wine or
    vermouth

2 shallots, finely chopped
2 tablespoons all-purpose flour
3 tablespoons butter
1/4 cup heavy cream
1 1/2 cups seedless grapes

Season the fish with the salt and white pepper. Place the fish in a saucepan with 3 tablespoons butter, the wine and shallots. Bring to a boil and reduce the heat. Simmer for 10 minutes. Remove the fish to an ovenproof serving dish, reserving the wine liquid in the saucepan.

Mix 2 tablespoons flour with 3 tablespoons butter and stir into the reserved wine liquid. Cook until smooth and thickened, stirring constantly. Stir in the cream.

Place the grapes over the fish and cover with the sauce. Broil until golden brown.

Serves 6

Fish Tacos

WHITE SAUCE

1/2 cup mayonnaise
1/2 cup plain yogurt or sour cream
1 tablespoon chopped cilantro
1 tablespoon lime juice

FRIED TILAPIA

1 pound tilapia or other
  white fish fillets
Salt to taste
1 cup all-purpose flour
1/2 teaspoon garlic powder
1/4 teaspoon cayenne pepper
1/4 teaspoon white pepper

1/4 teaspoon paprika
1 cup beer
Vegetable oil for frying

TACOS

1 head cabbage, shredded
1 tablespoon cider vinegar
1 teaspoon salt
12 corn tortillas
2 cups (8 ounces) shredded
  Cheddar cheese
1 ripe avocado, chopped
Mango salsa or hot salsa

To prepare the white sauce, combine the mayonnaise, yogurt, cilantro and lime juice in a bowl and mix well. Chill, covered, until ready to serve.

To prepare the fish, rinse the fish and dip in a bowl of lightly salted cold water. Drain and pat dry with paper towels. Mix the flour, garlic powder, cayenne pepper, white pepper, paprika and beer in a bowl until smooth. Coat the fish with the batter and deep-fry in 350-degree oil in a deep fryer until crisp and golden brown, keeping the fish apart while frying. Drain the fish on paper towels.

To prepare the tacos, combine the cabbage, cider vinegar and salt in a bowl and toss to mix. Heat the tortillas in a nonstick skillet until warm and light brown. Layer each tortilla with the white sauce, 1 fish fillet, the cabbage mixture, Cheddar cheese and avocado. Serve with the salsa for dipping.

Makes 1 dozen

Creole Tilapia

$1/2$ cup quick-cooking brown rice
1 onion, sliced
2 ribs celery, sliced
2 large carrots, sliced
2 tilapia fillets

1 cup canned diced tomatoes
2 tablespoons chopped fresh cilantro,
   parsley or basil
Seasoned salt to taste
Freshly ground pepper to taste

Prepare the rice using the package directions. Coat a large skillet with nonstick cooking spray. Sauté the onion, celery and carrots in the prepared skillet over medium-high heat for 5 minutes or until tender. Add the fish and cook for 3 minutes. Carefully turn the fish and add the tomatoes and cilantro. Season with salt and pepper. Simmer for 2 minutes or until the fish flakes easily with a fork. Serve over the rice.

Serves 2

Salmon Quiche

1 (15-ounce) can salmon
3 eggs, beaten, or an equivalent
   amount of egg substitute
1 cup sour cream
$1/4$ cup mayonnaise
3 drops of hot pepper sauce

$3/4$ cup (3 ounces) shredded
   Cheddar cheese
1 tablespoon chopped onion
$1/4$ teaspoon dried dill weed
2 unbaked (9-inch) pie shells

Drain the salmon, reserving the liquid. Add enough water to the reserved liquid to measure $1/2$ cup. Pour the liquid into a large bowl. Stir in the eggs, sour cream, mayonnaise and hot sauce. Add the salmon and stir to break into bite-size pieces. Stir in the Cheddar cheese, onion and dill weed. Spoon into the pie shells. Bake at 325 degrees for 40 to 45 minutes or until set, covering the edges with foil if needed to prevent overbrowning. Serve warm. (Note: For a crustless quiche, omit the pie shells and pour the filling into two 9-inch pie plates sprayed with nonstick cooking spray.)

Serves 12

Crab Casserole

6 green onions, chopped
4 garlic cloves, chopped
1/4 cup parsley, chopped
2 tablespoons minced green
   bell pepper
1/2 cup (1 stick) butter
1 teaspoon celery salt
8 slices bread, toasted until crisp

2 eggs, well beaten
2 pounds crab meat, shells
   removed and flaked
Half-and-half
Salt, black pepper and red pepper
   to taste
1 (15-ounce) can bread crumbs

Sauté the green onions, garlic, parsley and bell pepper in the butter in a skillet until soft. Season with the celery salt. Crumble the bread into small pieces and mix with the vegetable mixture. Add the eggs and mix well. Add the crab meat and enough half-and-half to moisten. Season with salt, black pepper and red pepper. Pour the mixture into a greased 3-quart baking dish. Cover the top with the bread crumbs. Bake at 375 degrees for 30 minutes.

Serves 10

Shrimp Bake

4 scallions, chopped
2 garlic cloves, finely chopped
2 tablespoons extra-virgin olive oil
1 (28-ounce) can chopped tomatoes
Freshly ground pepper to taste

2 pounds large (21- to 25-count)
   shrimp, peeled and deveined
1 cup crumbled feta cheese
2 tablespoons chopped fresh dill weed
   or oregano
Hot cooked rice

Sauté the scallions and garlic in the hot olive oil in a large ovenproof skillet over medium heat for 2 minutes or until the scallions become tender. Add the undrained tomatoes and bring to a boil. Cook for 5 minutes or until the juice begins to thicken. Season with freshly ground pepper. Remove from the heat and stir in the shrimp. Sprinkle with the feta cheese. Bake at 400 degrees for 10 minutes or until the feta cheese melts and the shrimp turn pink. Sprinkle with the dill weed and serve over hot cooked rice.

Serves 4

Sesame Orange Shrimp

2 egg whites
1/4 cup cornstarch
1/4 cup sesame seeds
1 teaspoon salt
1/2 teaspoon pepper
1 1/2 pounds medium shrimp,
    peeled and deveined
1/4 cup (or more) vegetable oil
1 cup fresh orange juice

2 tablespoons soy sauce
1 tablespoon sugar
4 scallions, trimmed and
    thinly sliced
2 garlic cloves, minced
2 tablespoons olive oil
2 large heads broccoli, trimmed
    into florets
Hot cooked rice

Whisk the egg whites, cornstarch, sesame seeds, salt and pepper in a small bowl until frothy. Add the shrimp and toss to coat. Heat 1/4 cup oil in a large nonstick skillet over medium-high heat. Cook the shrimp in two or three batches for 2 to 3 minutes per side or until crisp and golden, adding additional oil if needed. Remove the shrimp to paper towels to drain.

Wipe the skillet clean with a paper towel. Bring the orange juice, soy sauce and sugar to a boil in the skillet over high heat. Boil for 4 to 5 minutes or until the mixture is syrupy and reduced to about 1/3 cup. Return the shrimp to the skillet and add the scallions. Cook for 1 minute or until the shrimp are heated through and coated with the sauce.

Sauté the garlic in the olive oil in a sauté pan. Add the broccoli and sauté until tender. Serve the shrimp and broccoli with hot cooked rice.

Serves 4

JALAPEÑO LIME MARINADE

Remove the seeds from 2 jalapeño chiles. Mince the jalapeño chiles and place in a bowl. Add 1/2 cup thawed orange juice concentrate, 1/4 cup fresh lime juice, 2 teaspoons cumin, 3 garlic cloves, minced, 1 teaspoon grated lime zest, 1/4 cup honey and 1/4 teaspoon salt and stir to mix well. This is a wonderful marinade to use when grilling fish or shrimp. Makes 1 1/3 cups.

Shrimp in Sour Cream

1 1/2 pounds shrimp, peeled
  and deveined
2 shallots, minced
1/2 cup (1 stick) butter
8 ounces fresh mushrooms, sliced

2 tablespoons all-purpose flour
1 teaspoon salt
Pepper to taste
2 cups sour cream
1/4 cup sherry

Sauté the shrimp and shallots in half the butter in a skillet for 5 minutes or until the shrimp turn pink. Remove the shrimp from the skillet. Melt the remaining butter in the skillet. Add the mushrooms and sauté for 5 minutes. Blend in the flour, salt and pepper. Add the sour cream gradually and cook until thickened, stirring constantly. Return the shrimp to the skillet and heat until warm. Remove the skillet from the heat and stir in the wine.

Serves 4

Shrimp and Asparagus Pasta

7 garlic cloves, minced
1/4 teaspoon pepper
2 tablespoons olive oil
6 plum tomatoes, seeded
  and chopped
1/2 cup dry white wine
1/2 cup chicken broth
1 cup (1-inch) diagonally cut
  fresh asparagus pieces

1/4 teaspoon salt
12 ounces shrimp, cooked
  and peeled
2 tablespoons butter
9 ounces angel hair pasta,
  cooked and drained
12 fresh basil leaves,
  cut into strips

Sauté the garlic and pepper in the olive oil in a large saucepan over medium heat for 1 minute. Add the tomatoes and cook for 1 minute. Add the wine and chicken broth and simmer for 3 minutes or until the sauce is slightly reduced. Add the asparagus and salt. Cook for 3 minutes, stirring frequently. Stir in the shrimp. Cook for no longer than 1 minute, stirring constantly. Add the butter and heat until melted, stirring until well absorbed. Add the pasta and toss to coat. Stir in the basil. Remove to a serving platter or pasta bowl and serve.

Serves 2 or 3

Angel Hair Pasta with Pine Nuts

2 teaspoons minced garlic
1/4 cup olive oil
1/4 cup pine nuts, toasted
1/4 cup fresh lemon juice
1 tablespoon freshly grated
   lemon zest

1/2 cup flat-leaf parsley,
   minced
Salt and pepper to taste
8 ounces angel hair pasta

Sauté the garlic in the olive oil in a small saucepan over medium-high heat for 1 to 2 minutes or until softened. Spoon into a large pasta bowl. Add the pine nuts and crush lightly with the back of a fork. Stir in the lemon juice, lemon zest, parsley, salt and pepper.

Cook the pasta in boiling salted water in a large saucepan for 2 to 3 minutes or until al dente. Drain the pasta, reserving 2 tablespoons of the cooking liquid. Add the pasta and reserved cooking liquid to the lemon mixture and toss until the sauce is absorbed. Serve warm.

Serves 4

Linguini with Tomato and Basil

4 to 6 ripe tomatoes, cut into
   1/2-inch cubes
16 ounces crumbled feta cheese
1 cup fresh basil, cut into strips
3 to 5 garlic cloves, pressed
1 cup olive oil
1/2 teaspoon salt

1/2 teaspoon pepper
6 cups water
2 tablespoons olive oil
2 teaspoons salt
1 1/2 pounds linguini
Freshly grated Parmesan cheese

Combine the tomatoes, feta cheese, basil, garlic, 1 cup olive oil, 1/2 teaspoon salt and the pepper in a large bowl and stir to mix well. Cover and let stand at room temperature for 2 hours.

Bring the water, 2 tablespoons olive oil and 2 teaspoons salt to a boil in a large saucepan. Add the pasta and boil for 8 to 10 minutes or until firm yet tender; drain. Add to the tomato mixture and toss to coat. Sprinkle with Parmesan cheese. Serve immediately.

Serves 4

Main Dishes

Baking fish on a bed of celery and onions will add to the taste as well as keep the fish from sticking.

Scaling fish is easier if vinegar is rubbed on the scales first.

When cooking pasta, add a small amount of vegetable oil to the boiling water before adding the pasta to cut down on sticking.

To cook noodles, bring the required amount of water to a boil.
Add the noodles and then turn off the heat. Let stand for 20 minutes.
This method prevents over-boiling and the chore of stirring,
plus the noodles won't stick to the pan.

A roast with the bone will cook faster than a boneless roast because the bone carries heat to the inside more quickly.

Red wine used in cooking brings out the flavor of meat,
while white wine sweetens the flavor.

To tenderize tough meats or game, marinate in a mixture of equal parts vinegar and heated bouillon for 2 hours.

For best results when grilling foods, do not baste with butter or margarine until the last 15 to 20 minutes of grilling. Then you may baste with barbecue sauces or other sauces without their burning.

When cooking shrimp, add a few caraway seeds to the water to eliminate the odor while cooking.

If a dish lacks flavor, try adding a little mustard, hot pepper sauce, or Worcestershire sauce. An herb or spice such as curry powder can sometimes add too much flavor.

To keep the flavor in chicken, roast it in aluminum foil.
Basting is not required, and the cleanup is a breeze.

When preparing a casserole for freezing, line the baking dish with several layers of foil first before filling. The casserole can then be lifted out when frozen and wrapped for storage without losing the use of the baking dish. The casserole will stack easily in the freezer and will fit right back into the baking dish when it is time to bake.

Vegetables & Sides

"Vegetables are a must on a diet.
I suggest carrot cake, zucchini bread, and pumpkin pie."
—Garfield

"It's difficult to think anything but pleasant thoughts
while eating a homegrown tomato."
—Lewis Grizzard

"A fruit is a vegetable with looks and money. Plus, if you let fruit rot,
it turns into wine, something brussels sprouts never do."
—P. J. O'Rourke

"Life expectancy would grow by leaps and bounds if
green vegetables smelled as good as bacon."
—Doug Larson

Mushroom and Artichoke Casserole

1 pound fresh mushrooms, cut into halves	2 cups sour cream
6 tablespoons butter	1 teaspoon Worcestershire sauce
2 (6-ounce) cans artichoke hearts packed in water, rinsed and drained	Salt and pepper to taste
	Pinch of dried parsley
	1 cup bread crumbs

Sauté the mushrooms in the butter in a skillet for 10 minutes. Drain the mushrooms, reserving the liquid in the skillet. Layer the mushrooms and artichoke hearts in a baking dish. Stir the sour cream into the reserved liquid in the skillet. Add the Worcestershire sauce, salt, pepper and parsley. Pour over the artichoke hearts. Sprinkle with the bread crumbs. Bake at 350 degrees for 30 minutes.

Serves 6

Stuffed Artichokes

5 large artichokes, trimmed	1/4 cup (1/2 stick) butter
1/4 teaspoon salt	1 cup Italian bread crumbs
1 large onion, chopped	1 teaspoon grated Parmesan cheese
2 teaspoons minced garlic	1 tablespoon olive oil
3 tablespoons olive oil	

Place the artichokes and salt in a large saucepan and fill the saucepan with just enough water to cover the artichokes. Bring to a boil over high heat and cook for 35 to 40 minutes or until the artichokes are tender. Remove the artichokes and let drain upside down. Place in an 8×8-inch baking dish.

Sauté the onion and garlic in 3 tablespoons olive oil and the butter in a medium skillet over medium heat for 3 minutes or until the onion is tender. Remove from the heat and stir in the bread crumbs and Parmesan cheese. Spread the artichoke leaves apart and fill the spaces between the leaves with the stuffing mixture. Drizzle 1 tablespoon olive oil over the artichokes. Cover tightly with foil and bake at 375 degrees for 15 to 20 minutes or until hot. Serve immediately. (Note: To eat, pull off each artichoke leaf and eat only the pulp by removing it with your teeth. For added flavor, squeeze the juice of 1/2 lemon into the boiling water with the artichokes.)

Serves 4

Hazelnut Parmesan Asparagus

1 1/2 pounds asparagus spears
2 tablespoons butter
2 1/2 cups sliced mushrooms
1 1/2 teaspoons chopped fresh basil
  leaves, or 1/2 teaspoon dried
  basil leaves

1/4 teaspoon salt
1/4 teaspoon coarsely ground pepper
Juice of 1/2 lemon
1 cup (4 ounces) shredded
  Parmesan cheese
1/4 cup hazelnuts, chopped

Snap off the tough ends of the asparagus and rinse under cool water. Place a 10-inch ovenproof skillet in a 500-degree oven for 5 minutes. Remove from the oven and maintain the oven temperature. Swirl the butter in the hot skillet until melted. Add the asparagus and mushrooms to the melted butter, tossing to coat. Add the basil, salt and pepper and mix to coat. Sprinkle with the lemon juice. Bake for 5 to 10 minutes or until the asparagus is tender-crisp. Remove to a serving platter and sprinkle with the Parmesan cheese and hazelnuts.

Serves 8

Broccoli Casserole

1 cup mayonnaise
1 (10-ounce) can celery soup
2 eggs, lightly beaten
1 cup (4 ounces) shredded sharp
  Cheddar cheese
2 tablespoons minced onion
1 tablespoon Worcestershire sauce

Salt and pepper to taste
2 (10-ounce) packages frozen
  chopped broccoli, cooked
  and drained
2 cups cracker crumbs
2 tablespoons butter, melted

Mix the mayonnaise, soup, eggs, Cheddar cheese, onion, Worcestershire sauce, salt and pepper in a bowl. Fold in the broccoli. Spoon into a greased 9×13-inch baking dish. Sprinkle the cracker crumbs evenly over the top. Pour the melted butter evenly over the crackers. Bake at 325 degrees for 45 minutes or until set and brown.

Serves 8

AVOCADO BUTTER

Peel and seed 1 fresh avocado. Process the avocado in a food processor until smooth. Add 1/4 cup mayonnaise, 2 tablespoons lemon juice, 1/4 teaspoon salt and 1/16 teaspoon pepper and blend well. Fold in 1 chopped hard-cooked egg. Serve over steamed asparagus or fresh green beans. Makes 1 cup.

Root Beer Baked Beans

3 bacon slices
1 small onion, chopped
2 (16-ounce) cans pork and beans
$1/2$ cup root beer

$1/4$ cup hickory-smoked
  barbecue sauce
$1/2$ teaspoon dry mustard
$1/8$ teaspoon hot pepper sauce

Cook the bacon in a large skillet until crisp. Drain the bacon, reserving
2 tablespoons of the bacon drippings in the skillet. Crumble the bacon. Sauté
the onion in the reserved bacon drippings for 5 minutes. Add the pork and
beans, root beer, barbecue sauce, dry mustard and hot pepper sauce and mix
well. Stir in the crumbled bacon. Spoon into a greased 1-quart baking dish.
Bake at 400 degrees for 55 minutes or until thickened.

Serves 6

Easy Green Bean–Bacon Bundles

1 pound fresh green beans
8 thin bacon slices
$1/3$ cup butter

$1/2$ cup packed brown sugar
1 garlic clove, minced

Boil the green beans in boiling water to cover in a saucepan for 5 to 7 minutes
or until tender-crisp. Drain and blanch in ice water to stop the cooking process.
Arrange the green beans in eight bundles. Wrap each bundle with a slice of the
bacon and secure with a wooden pick. Place in a baking dish sprayed with
nonstick cooking spray.

Melt the butter in a saucepan. Add the brown sugar and heat until dissolved,
stirring constantly. Stir in the garlic. Pour over the green bean bundles. Bake at
325 degrees for 25 to 30 minutes or until the brown sugar mixture is bubbly.
Broil for 3 to 5 minutes or until the bacon is crisp.

Serves 8

Carrot Soufflé

SOUFFLÉ

2 cups mashed cooked carrots

3 eggs

2 tablespoons all-purpose flour

$1/2$ cup sugar

$1/2$ cup heavy cream

$1/4$ cup ($1/2$ stick) butter, softened

1 teaspoon vanilla extract

$1/4$ teaspoon ground nutmeg

$1/4$ teaspoon ground cinnamon

PECAN TOPPING

1 cup granulated sugar

$1/2$ cup (1 stick) butter

1 cup pecans, chopped

$1/2$ teaspoon ground nutmeg

$1/2$ teaspoon ground cinnamon

$1/3$ cup all-purpose flour

Confectioners' sugar

To prepare the soufflé, process the carrots, eggs, flour, sugar, cream, butter, vanilla, nutmeg and cinnamon in a blender or food processor until smooth. Spoon into a greased baking dish.

To prepare the topping, mix the granulated sugar, butter, pecans, nutmeg, cinnamon and flour in a bowl until crumbly. Sprinkle over the soufflé. Bake at 350 degrees for 35 minutes or until set. Dust very lightly with confectioners' sugar before serving.

Serves 6

GRILLED CABBAGE

Cut out the core of one head of cabbage, making a lid with the core. Season the center of the cabbage with garlic, salt, black pepper and cayenne pepper to taste. Add 2 tablespoons butter to the center. Pour half a can of light beer into the center and replace the core lid. Wrap completely in several layers of foil and place on a grill rack. Grill over medium heat for 1 hour. Serves 4.

Creamed Corn

1 cup half-and-half
1 (16-ounce) package frozen
   corn, thawed
1/4 cup sugar
1 teaspoon salt

Pinch of white pepper
Cornstarch
3/4 cup (3 ounces) grated
   Parmesan cheese

Bring the half-and-half to a boil in a saucepan. Reduce the heat and stir in the corn. Simmer for 5 minutes. Stir in the sugar, salt and white pepper. Remove from the heat and gradually stir in enough cornstarch to thicken to a soupy consistency. Pour into a 9×13-inch baking dish and cover with the Parmesan cheese. Broil for 2 to 3 minutes or until the top is golden brown.

Serves 4 to 6

Indian Eggplant

1 large eggplant, quartered
1 large onion, chopped
Vegetable oil
2 or 3 tomatoes, chopped

Salt to taste
1 or 2 red chiles, chopped, or
   red chile powder to taste

Place the eggplant in a microwave-safe dish. Microwave on High for 10 to 15 minutes or until the eggplant is soft enough to scoop out of the peel. Place the eggplant in a bowl and chop or mash. Sauté the onion in vegetable oil in a skillet until translucent. Add the tomatoes, salt and red chiles. Stir in the eggplant. Simmer for 5 minutes or until heated through.

Serves 4

CAJUN RUB FOR CORN ON THE COB

Combine 1 tablespoon salt, 1/2 tablespoon garlic powder, 1/2 tablespoon cayenne pepper, 3/4 teaspoon white pepper, 3/4 teaspoon black pepper, 3/4 teaspoon basil, 3/4 teaspoon thyme and 1/2 teaspoon oregano in a sealable plastic bag. Seal the bag and shake well to mix. Coat buttered cooked corn on the cob with the rub and garnish with chopped fresh parsley. Makes 1/2 cup.

Cider Scalloped Potatoes

2 tablespoons all-purpose flour
1 cup low-fat milk
1 cup apple cider
1/2 cup fat-free chicken broth
1/2 teaspoon salt
1/4 teaspoon pepper
1/8 teaspoon ground nutmeg

1/2 cup (2 ounces) shredded
   smoked Gouda cheese
1/2 cup (2 ounces) shredded
   low-fat Jarlsberg cheese
2 pounds Yukon gold potatoes,
   peeled and thinly sliced

Place the flour in a medium saucepan. Whisk in the milk gradually until blended. Stir in the cider, chicken broth, salt, pepper and nutmeg. Bring to a boil over medium heat, stirring constantly. Mix the Gouda cheese and Jarlsberg cheese in a small bowl. Reserve 1/2 cup of the cheese mixture for the topping. Layer one-half of the potatoes, the remaining cheese mixture and remaining potatoes in a greased baking dish. Pour the cider mixture over the potatoes. Bake at 425 degrees for 25 minutes. Remove from the oven and press the potatoes with a spatula. Sprinkle with the reserved cheese mixture. Bake for 20 minutes or until the potatoes are tender. Let stand for 10 minutes before serving.

Serves 8

Jalapeño and Corn Mashed Potatoes

12 ounces cream cheese, cubed
5 tablespoons butter
1/4 cup milk
5 cups mashed potatoes
1 1/2 cups corn, cooked and drained

3 or 4 jalapeño chiles, seeded
   and minced
2 teaspoons salt
2 teaspoons white pepper

Melt the cream cheese and butter in the milk in a saucepan over low heat. Stir into the mashed potatoes. Add the corn, jalapeño chiles, salt and white pepper and mix well. Spoon into a buttered 9×13-inch baking dish. Bake at 350 degrees for 3 to 5 minutes or until the top is golden brown. (Note: Wear gloves when handling the fresh jalapeño chiles as the oils may cause skin irritation.)

Serves 6

Totally Sinful Potatoes

1 pound sliced bacon
5 pounds red potatoes
1 tablespoon liquid crab boil,
  or to taste
1 pound Velveeta cheese, cubed

2 cups sour cream
5 green onions, chopped
1 cup (2 sticks) butter
Salt and pepper to taste

Cook the bacon in a skillet until crisp. Drain the bacon, reserving 2 tablespoons of the bacon drippings. Crumble the bacon into small pieces.

Cut the red potatoes into quarters, leaving the skins on. Place in a large saucepan of boiling water. Add the liquid crab boil and cook until the red potatoes are fork-tender. Drain and return to the saucepan. Add the bacon, Velveeta cheese, sour cream, green onions, butter and reserved bacon drippings and stir until the red potatoes are mashed but still chunky. Season with salt and pepper.

Serves 10 to 12

Whipped Sweet Potatoes and Carrots

3 pounds sweet potatoes, peeled
  and cut into 1-inch pieces
2 chicken bouillon cubes
4 carrots, peeled and cut into
  1-inch pieces

6 tablespoons unsalted butter
1/4 cup packed light brown sugar
2 tablespoons fresh orange juice
Salt to taste

Place the sweet potatoes and bouillon cubes in a large heavy saucepan and cover with cold water. Bring to a boil and reduce the heat. Simmer for 15 minutes or until very tender. Drain the sweet potatoes, reserving 6 tablespoons of the cooking liquid.

Place the carrots in a saucepan and cover with cold water. Bring to a boil and reduce the heat. Simmer for 20 to 25 minutes or until tender; drain. Purée the carrots in a food processor.

Mash the sweet potatoes with the reserved cooking liquid in a bowl. Add the puréed carrots, butter, brown sugar, orange juice and salt and mix well. Serve immediately or reheat, covered, in a 350-degree oven for 15 to 20 minutes or until heated through.

Serves 8 to 10

Spinach and Cheese Soufflé

2 (10-ounce) packages chopped
   frozen spinach
1/4 cup (1/2 stick) butter, melted
1/4 cup all-purpose flour
3 eggs

12 ounces cottage cheese
Salt and pepper to taste
1 1/3 cups Cheddar cheese cubes
1 1/3 cups Monterey Jack
   cheese cubes

Cook the spinach using the package directions; drain. Pat the spinach dry with paper towels and set aside. Pour the melted butter into a bowl and gradually add the flour, blending until smooth. Add the spinach, eggs, cottage cheese, salt and pepper and mix well. Stir in the Cheddar cheese cubes and Monterey Jack cheese cubes. Spoon into a greased 2-quart baking dish. Bake at 350 degrees for 1 hour.

Serves 6

Squash Casserole

2/3 cup chopped green onions
1 cup julienned green bell pepper
3 tablespoons butter, melted
2 cups grated carrots
3 tablespoons chopped parsley
2 pounds yellow squash, sliced
   (about 6 cups)

1 teaspoon salt
Pepper to taste
1 teaspoon crushed dried
   sweet basil
1 cup sour cream
1 cup (4 ounces) grated
   Parmesan cheese

Sauté the green onions and bell pepper in the melted butter in a skillet for 3 minutes. Add the carrots and parsley and sauté for 3 minutes. Add the squash and sauté for 3 minutes. Season with the salt, pepper and basil. Fold in the sour cream and Parmesan cheese. Spoon into a 3-quart baking dish. Bake at 350 degrees for 30 to 40 minutes or until heated through.

Serves 6

SUMMER MEAL

Combine 2 cups chopped okra, 2 cups sliced yellow squash, 2 cups sliced uncooked potatoes, 1 cup sliced onion, 1/2 cup yellow cornmeal and salt and pepper to taste in a large bowl and toss until evenly coated. Fry in hot vegetable oil in a large skillet over medium heat until golden brown. Serves 6.

Herbed Butter Zucchini Fans

1/3 cup butter, softened
1 tablespoon olive oil
2 tablespoons minced fresh parsley
1/4 teaspoon dried tarragon
1/8 teaspoon salt
1/8 teaspoon pepper

4 small zucchini
 (about 6 inches long)
1/4 cup water
2 tablespoons freshly grated
 Parmesan cheese
1 tablespoon soft bread crumbs

Mix the butter, olive oil, parsley, tarragon, salt and pepper in a bowl. Cut each zucchini lengthwise into 4 thick slices down to within 1/2 inch of the stem; do not cut all the way through. Fan the slices out and spread evenly with the herbed butter. Place in a large baking pan and add the water. Bake at 400 degrees for 20 minutes or until tender-crisp, basting several times with the herbed butter. Mix the Parmesan cheese and bread crumbs in a bowl. Sprinkle the zucchini fans with the bread crumb mixture. Broil 4 inches from the heat source for 1 to 2 minutes or until the Parmesan cheese is melted and golden brown.

Serves 4

Green Chile Hominy

10 slices bacon
1 cup chopped onion
4 (15-ounce) cans white hominy
1 tablespoon jalapeño juice

8 ounces Cheddar cheese, shredded
1 cup chopped green chiles
1 or 2 pickled jalapeño chiles,
 seeded and chopped (optional)

Fry the bacon in a skillet until crisp. Drain the bacon, reserving a small amount of the bacon drippings. Crumble the bacon into pieces. Sauté the onion in the reserved bacon drippings in the skillet. Drain the hominy, reserving 1/2 cup of the liquid. Heat the hominy in a sauté pan until heated through, stirring frequently. Add the reserved hominy liquid and jalapeño juice. Increase the heat to high and add three-fourths of the Cheddar cheese. Heat until the cheese melts. Add one-half of the green chiles, one-half of the jalapeño chiles, one-half of the bacon and all of the sautéed onion and mix well. Spoon into a 9×13-inch baking dish. Sprinkle with the remaining cheese, bacon, green chiles and jalapeño chiles. Bake at 325 degrees for 15 minutes or until the cheese melts. (This dish may be made ahead and chilled or frozen before baking. Bake for 40 minutes or until the cheese melts.)

Serves 10 to 12

Homemade Macaroni and Cheese Bake

1/2 cup (2 ounces) shredded Muenster cheese	1 pound elbow macaroni
1/2 cup (2 ounces) shredded mild Cheddar cheese	1/2 cup (1 stick) butter, melted
	2 cups half-and-half
1/2 cup (2 ounces) shredded sharp Cheddar cheese	1 cup small Velveeta cheese cubes
	2 eggs, lightly beaten
1/2 cup (2 ounces) shredded Monterey Jack cheese	1/4 teaspoon salt
	1/8 teaspoon pepper
	1 tablespoon butter

Combine the Muenster cheese, mild Cheddar cheese, sharp Cheddar cheese and Monterey Jack cheese in a bowl and mix well. Cook the macaroni in a large saucepan using the package directions; drain. Stir 1/2 cup butter into the hot macaroni. Add the half-and-half, 1 1/2 cups of the cheese mixture, the Velveeta cheese cubes and eggs and mix well. Season with the salt and pepper. Spoon into a lightly buttered deep 2 1/2-quart baking dish. Sprinkle with the remaining 1/2 cup cheese mixture. Dot with 1 tablespoon butter. Bake at 350 degrees for 35 minutes.

Serves 4 to 6

LEMON DRESSING

Combine 1/4 cup lemon juice, 1/4 cup vegetable oil, 1 teaspoon sugar, 1/2 teaspoon salt, 1/4 teaspoon paprika, 1 tablespoon finely chopped onion and 1 garlic clove, crushed, in a jar with a tight-fitting lid. Seal the jar and shake to mix well. Let stand at room temperature for several hours before serving. Shake well before serving and pour over hot cooked vegetables such as asparagus, broccoli or green beans. Serves 8.

Spicy Monterey Rice

2 cups water
1 cup uncooked long grain rice
1 tablespoon chicken instant bouillon granules, or
    3 chicken bouillon cubes
2 cups sour cream
1 or 2 (4-ounce) cans chopped green chiles
1/2 cup chopped red bell pepper (optional)
1/8 teaspoon pepper
1 cup (4 ounces) shredded Colby cheese
1 cup (4 ounces) shredded Monterey Jack cheese
1/2 cup (2 ounces) shredded Colby cheese

Combine the water, rice and bouillon granules in a medium saucepan and bring to a boil. Reduce the heat and simmer for 15 minutes or until the rice is tender. Combine the rice, sour cream, undrained green chiles, bell pepper and pepper and mix well. Stir in 1 cup Colby cheese and the Monterey Jack cheese. Spoon into a buttered 1 1/2-quart baking dish. Bake at 350 degrees for 20 to 25 minutes or until heated through. Sprinkle with 1/2 cup Colby cheese and bake for 3 minutes or until the cheese melts. Store any leftovers in the refrigerator. (Note: You may substitute sharp Cheddar cheese, three-cheese Mexican blend or any cheese of choice for the Colby cheese or Monterey Jack cheese.)

Serves 6 to 10

HELPFUL HINTS

Vegetables & Sides

To keep asparagus its freshest, wrap the bases of the fresh asparagus spears in wet paper towels and keep tightly sealed in a storage container in the refrigerator for up to 4 days.

To prepare vegetables in advance, blanch, drain, and rinse under cold water to stop further cooking. Wrap the vegetables and refrigerate. At serving time, drop the blanched vegetables into boiling water for 30 seconds to reheat, and then toss with flavored butter.

To make celery more crisp, place it in a bowl of water and add ice. Chill in the refrigerator for a few hours.

Add a little milk while cooking cauliflower to keep it bright white.

To roast peppers, broil the whole pepper with tops 5 inches from the heat source until the skin is blistered and evenly browned but not burned, turning occasionally. Place the peppers in a plastic bag and let stand for 20 minutes. Peel the skin from the peppers before using.

To store a cut avocado, allow the seed to remain embedded and spread the edges with mayonnaise, soft butter or cream. Cover well with waxed paper or plastic wrap and chill in the refrigerator.

When cooking canned vegetables, drain the liquid from the vegetables into a saucepan. Bring to a boil and cook until the liquid is reduced to about $1/3$ or $1/2$ cup. Add the vegetables and seasonings and cook until heated through.

Add a teaspoon of lemon juice to each quart of water used to cook rice. The grains will stay white and separated.

White rice keeps almost indefinitely on the shelf. Store white rice in a tightly covered container. It's best to store brown rice and wild rice in the refrigerator since the oils can turn rancid.

Drain and lightly rinse canned beans to remove excess salt before using.

Potatoes will roast in half the time if they are boiled for 5 minutes and then placed in a hot oven.

Desserts

"*When baking, follow directions.
When cooking, go by your own taste.*"

—Laiko Bahrs

"*Part of the secret of success in life is to eat what you like
and let the food fight it out inside.*"

—Mark Twain

"*Avoid fruits and nuts...remember you are what you eat.*"

—Jim Davis

"*Everything I eat has been proved by some doctor or other
to be a deadly poison, and everything I don't eat has been proved to be
indispensable for life. But I go marching on.*"

—George Bernard Shaw

Pumpkin Cheesecake

1/2 cup gingersnap cookie crumbs
1/2 cup walnuts or pecans, chopped
16 ounces cream cheese, softened
1 1/2 cups sugar
6 eggs, at room temperature
1/3 cup all-purpose flour
1 1/2 teaspoons ground cinnamon

1 teaspoon ground nutmeg
1 teaspoon ground cloves
1/4 teaspoon ground allspice
1/8 teaspoon salt
2 cups pumpkin purée
Whipped cream (optional)

Combine the cookie crumbs and walnuts in a bowl and mix well. Sprinkle in a buttered 9-inch springform pan and chill in the refrigerator. Beat the cream cheese, sugar, eggs, flour, cinnamon, nutmeg, cloves, allspice and salt in a mixing bowl until smooth. Add the pumpkin purée and blend well. Spoon into the prepared pan. Bake at 325 degrees for 1 1/2 hours. Turn off the oven and let stand in the oven with the door ajar for 30 minutes. Remove to a wire rack to cool. Chill until ready to serve. Cut into slices and serve with whipped cream.

Serves 8 to 12

Sopaipilla Cheesecake

2 (8-count) cans crescent rolls
16 ounces cream cheese, softened
1 cup sugar
1 teaspoon vanilla extract

1/2 cup (1 stick) butter, softened
3/4 cup sugar
1 tablespoon ground cinnamon

Unroll 1 can of the crescent roll dough, pressing the perforations to seal. Place the dough in a greased 9×13-inch baking pan. Beat the cream cheese, 1 cup sugar and the vanilla in a mixing bowl until smooth. Spread over the crescent roll dough layer. Unroll the remaining can of crescent roll dough, pressing the perforations to seal. Place over the cream cheese layer. Cream the butter and 3/4 cup sugar in a mixing bowl until light and fluffy. Spread over the top of the crescent roll dough. Sprinkle with the cinnamon. Bake at 350 degrees for 30 minutes.

Serves 12

Coffee Angel Food Cake with Coffee Frosting

CAKE
1 package white angel food cake mix
1 tablespoon instant coffee granules

COFFEE FROSTING
3/4 cup (1 1/2 sticks) butter, softened
1/4 teaspoon salt
3 3/4 cups confectioners' sugar
1 1/2 teaspoons vanilla extract
4 to 6 tablespoons milk
2 tablespoons instant coffee granules

ASSEMBLY
Sliced almonds

To prepare the cake, prepare the cake mix and bake using the package directions, adding 1 tablespoon instant coffee granules. Cool using the package directions.

To prepare the frosting, beat the butter, salt and confectioners' sugar in a mixing bowl until light and fluffy. Add the vanilla, milk and coffee granules and beat until the frosting is light.

To assemble, invert the cake onto a cake plate. Spread the frosting over the top and side of the cake. Place the almonds on the top and side of the cake.

Serves 12

Nutmeg Chiffon Cake with Browned Butter Icing

CAKE

2 1/4 cups cake flour, sifted
1 1/2 cups sugar
1 tablespoon baking powder
1 1/4 teaspoons ground nutmeg
1/2 teaspoon salt
7 egg yolks, at room temperature
1/2 cup vegetable oil
3/4 cup cold water
7 egg whites, at room temperature
1/2 teaspoon cream of tartar

BROWNED BUTTER ICING

3 tablespoons butter
2 cups confectioners' sugar, sifted
1 teaspoon vanilla extract
3 to 4 tablespoons milk

ASSEMBLY

1/4 cup sliced almonds or chopped
   nuts of choice

To prepare the cake, mix the cake flour, sugar, baking powder, nutmeg and salt together in a large mixing bowl. Make a well in the center and add the egg yolks, oil and cold water. Beat at low or medium speed until the mixture is combined. Beat at high speed for 4 to 5 minutes or until satin smooth. Thoroughly wash and dry the beaters. Beat the egg whites and cream of tartar at medium speed in a large mixing bowl until stiff peaks form. Add the egg yolk mixture in a thin stream, folding in gently. Pour the batter into an ungreased 10-inch tube pan. Place the pan on a baking sheet. Bake at 325 degrees for 60 to 65 minutes or until the top springs back when lightly touched. Invert onto a funnel to cool completely.

To prepare the icing, heat the butter in a saucepan for 15 minutes or until brown. Remove from the heat. Combine the confectioners' sugar, melted butter and vanilla in a medium bowl and mix well. Stir in enough milk to make of the desired spreading consistency.

To assemble, loosen the cake from the side of the pan. Invert onto a cake plate and frost with the icing. Garnish with the almonds.

Serves 12

Chocolate Chip Applesauce Cake

2 cups all-purpose flour
2 tablespoons baking cocoa
1 1/2 teaspoons baking soda
1/2 teaspoon salt
1/2 teaspoon ground cinnamon
1/2 cup (1 stick) butter, softened

1 cup sugar
2 eggs
2 cups applesauce
2 tablespoons sugar
1 cup (6 ounces) chocolate chips

Mix the flour, baking cocoa, baking soda, salt and cinnamon together. Cream the butter and 1 cup sugar in a mixing bowl until light and fluffy. Add the eggs and mix well. Add the flour mixture and applesauce alternately, beating well after each addition. Pour into a greased and floured 9×12-inch cake pan. Sprinkle with 2 tablespoons sugar and the chocolate chips. Bake at 350 degrees for 30 minutes.

Serves 12

Grand Marnier Cake

2 cups all-purpose flour
1 teaspoon baking powder
1 teaspoon baking soda
1 cup (2 sticks) butter, softened
1 cup sugar
3 egg yolks
1 teaspoon Grand Marnier or
    other orange liqueur

1 1/4 cups sour cream
Grated zest of 1 orange
1 cup walnuts, chopped
3 egg whites, stiffly beaten
1/2 cup sugar
1 cup orange juice
1/3 cup Grand Marnier

Sift the flour, baking powder and baking soda together. Cream the butter and 1 cup sugar in a mixing bowl until light and fluffy. Beat in the egg yolks one at a time. Add 1 teaspoon Grand Marnier. Add the flour mixture and sour cream alternately, beating until smooth after each addition. Stir in the orange zest and walnuts. Fold in the stiffly beaten egg whites. Pour into a greased bundt pan. Bake at 350 degrees for 45 to 50 minutes or until a wooden pick inserted in the center comes out clean. Remove from the oven and poke holes with wooden picks in the top of the hot cake. Combine 1/2 cup sugar, the orange juice and 1/3 cup Grand Marnier in a bowl and mix well. Pour over the hot cake. Let stand until cool. Invert the cake onto a serving plate.

Serves 12

Happy Day Cake with Orange Glaze

CAKE

2 1/2 cups all-purpose flour, sifted

1 1/2 cups sugar

1 tablespoon baking powder

1 teaspoon salt

1/2 cup shortening,
   at room temperature

3/4 cup milk

1 teaspoon vanilla extract

1/4 cup milk

2 eggs

ORANGE GLAZE

1 cup confectioners' sugar

1 tablespoon rum

2 teaspoons grated orange zest

Dash of salt

2 to 3 teaspoons hot water

ASSEMBLY

1 cup orange marmalade

To prepare the cake, line two 9-inch cake pans with waxed paper and grease well. Sift the flour, sugar, baking powder and salt together. Place the shortening in a mixing bowl and stir until softened. Add the flour mixture, 3/4 cup milk and the vanilla and mix until the flour mixture is dampened. Beat at medium speed for 2 minutes. Add 1/4 cup milk and beat well. Add the eggs one at a time, beating well after each addition. Pour into the prepared cake pans. Bake at 350 degrees for 25 to 30 minutes or until a cake tester inserted in the center comes out clean. Cool in the pans for 10 minutes. Invert onto wire racks to cool completely.

To prepare the glaze, combine the confectioners' sugar, rum, orange zest and salt in a bowl and mix well. Stir in enough hot water to make a thin glaze.

To assemble, spread the orange marmalade between the cake layers. Punch holes in the top of the cake with a wooden pick. Drizzle the glaze over the top of the cake.

Serves 12 to 15

Kahlúa Cake

CAKE

1 (2-layer) package chocolate
    fudge cake mix
1 (6-ounce) package chocolate
    instant pudding mix
2 eggs
2 cups sour cream
1/2 cup vegetable oil
1/3 cup Kahlúa or other
    coffee-flavored liqueur
1 cup (6 ounces) chocolate chips

KAHLÚA ICING

1 cup confectioners' sugar, sifted
2 tablespoons Kahlúa or other
    coffee-flavored liqueur
1 tablespoon hot coffee
Water

To prepare the cake, combine the cake mix, pudding mix, eggs, sour cream, oil and Kahlúa in a mixing bowl and mix well. Beat for 2 minutes longer. Fold in the chocolate chips. Pour into a well-greased bundt pan. Bake at 350 degrees for 45 to 50 minutes or until the cake tests done. Remove from the oven and cool in the pan for 10 minutes. Invert the cake onto a cake plate to cool completely.

To prepare the icing, combine the confectioners' sugar, Kahlúa and hot coffee in a bowl and mix well. Add enough water to make a thick syrupy consistency. Drizzle over the cooled cake.

Serves 12

KAHLÚA

To make homemade Kahlúa, boil 4 cups water, 2 cups granulated sugar and 2 cups packed brown sugar in a saucepan for 20 minutes, stirring constantly. Stir in 1/4 cup freeze-dried coffee granules and cool for 5 minutes. The mixture may appear slightly lumpy. Pour into a one-gallon jug. Add 1 liter of vodka and 1 vanilla bean and shake well. Shake once a day for 10 days. Makes 1 gallon.

Honey Bun Cake

CAKE

1 (2-layer) package moist butter
    recipe yellow cake mix

1 cup (2 sticks) butter, softened

4 eggs

1 cup sour cream

$1/2$ cup packed brown sugar

$1/3$ cup chopped pecans

2 teaspoons ground cinnamon

VANILLA GLAZE

1 cup confectioners' sugar

1 tablespoon (or more) milk

1 teaspoon vanilla extract

To prepare the cake, generously grease the bottom of a 9×13-inch cake pan. Reserve $1/2$ cup of the dry cake mix. Combine the remaining cake mix, butter, eggs and sour cream in a large mixing bowl and beat at medium speed for 2 minutes, scraping the bowl occasionally. Spread one-half of the batter in the prepared pan. Mix the reserved cake mix, brown sugar, pecans and cinnamon in a small bowl. Sprinkle over the batter. Drop the remaining batter by dollops over the pecan mixture and carefully spread to cover. Bake at 350 degrees for 40 to 45 minutes or until the cake is a deep golden brown and springs back when lightly touched.

To prepare the glaze, mix the confectioners' sugar, 1 tablespoon milk and the vanilla in a bowl until thin enough to drizzle, adding additional milk 1 teaspoon at a time if needed. Poke several holes in the top of the warm cake with a fork. Spread the glaze over the top of the cake. Let stand for 1 hour to cool completely and then cover to store.

Serves 12

POUND CAKE TIP

When baking a pound cake, butter the bottom of the cake pan and sprinkle with sugar before pouring in the batter. This will make a beautiful sparkling top when you invert the pound cake.

Poppy Seed Cake

1/2 cup sugar

1 tablespoon ground cinnamon

1 (2-layer) package white cake mix
  or yellow cake mix

1 (6-ounce) package French
  vanilla instant pudding mix

5 eggs

1 cup orange juice

1/2 cup vegetable oil

1/4 cup poppy seeds

Mix the sugar and cinnamon together. Grease a bundt pan and coat with the cinnamon-sugar. Combine the cake mix, pudding mix, eggs, orange juice and oil in a large mixing bowl and beat at low speed for 30 seconds or until moistened. Beat at medium speed for 2 minutes, scraping the side of the bowl. Add the poppy seeds and mix until incorporated. Pour into the prepared pan. Bake at 350 degrees for 35 to 45 minutes or until the cake tests done. Cool in the pan for 10 minutes. Invert onto a wire rack to cool completely.

Serves 12

Cream Cheese Pound Cake

3 cups all-purpose flour, sifted

1/8 teaspoon salt

1 1/2 cups (3 sticks) butter,
  softened

8 ounces cream cheese, softened

3 cups sugar

6 eggs

1 tablespoon vanilla extract

Mix the flour and salt together. Beat the butter and cream cheese at medium speed in a mixing bowl until creamy. Add the sugar gradually, beating constantly. Add the eggs one at a time, beating until combined after each addition. Stir in the vanilla. Add the flour mixture gradually, beating at low speed just until blended. Do not overbeat. Pour into a greased and floured bundt pan. Bake at 300 degrees for 1 hour and 40 minutes. Cool the cake in the pan on a wire rack for 15 minutes. Invert the cake onto the wire rack to cool completely.

Serves 12

Red Velvet Cake

CAKE

2 cups all-purpose flour
1 tablespoon baking cocoa
1 teaspoon salt
1 1/2 cups sugar
1/2 cup shortening
2 eggs
1 cup buttermilk
1 ounce red food coloring
1 teaspoon vanilla extract
1 teaspoon baking soda
1 tablespoon apple cider vinegar

BUTTER FROSTING

1/4 cup plus 1 tablespoon
  all-purpose flour
1/4 teaspoon salt
1 cup milk
1 cup (2 sticks) butter,
  softened
1 cup sugar
2 teaspoons vanilla extract

ASSEMBLY

1 cup flaked coconut

To prepare the cake, sift the flour, baking cocoa and salt together three times. Combine the sugar, shortening and eggs in a large bowl and beat well. Add the flour mixture and buttermilk alternately, beating well after each addition. Stir in the food coloring and vanilla. Fold in the baking soda and apple cider vinegar; do not beat. Pour into two greased and floured 9-inch cake pans. Bake at 350 degrees for 20 to 25 minutes or until the centers spring back when lightly touched and the cake pulls from the side of the pans. Cool in the pans for 10 minutes. Invert onto wire racks to cool completely.

To prepare the frosting, combine the flour, salt and milk in a saucepan and mix until blended. Cook until thickened, stirring constantly. Remove from the heat to cool. Cream the butter and sugar in a mixing bowl until fluffy. Add the cooled milk mixture and beat well. Beat in the vanilla.

To assemble, cut the cake layers horizontally into halves to create four layers. Spread some of the frosting between the layers, sprinkling each layer with the coconut. Spread the remaining frosting over the top and side of the cake.

Serves 12 to 15

Southern Bourbon Balls

3 cups vanilla wafers
1 cup pecans
1 cup confectioners' sugar
1/2 cup baking cocoa
1/8 teaspoon ground cinnamon
1/2 cup bourbon

3 tablespoons light corn syrup
1/2 teaspoon vanilla extract
Confectioners' sugar, baking cocoa
  or finely shredded coconut
  for coating

Grind the vanilla wafers in a food processor to form a fine dust. Spoon into a large bowl. Grind the pecans in a food processor until finely chopped. Add the pecans, 1 cup confectioners' sugar, the baking cocoa and cinnamon to the vanilla wafer dust and mix well. Blend the bourbon, corn syrup and vanilla in a liquid measure. Stir into the dry mixture until thoroughly combined. Press and roll the mixture into 1-inch balls. Roll each ball in confectioners' sugar to coat. Store in a tightly covered container at room temperature for 3 days before serving.

Makes 3 to 4 dozen

Martha Washington Jets

1 (16-ounce) package
  confectioners' sugar
1/2 cup (1 stick) butter, softened
1 tablespoon cream or
  half-and-half

1 teaspoon vanilla extract
1 (8-ounce) bar semisweet chocolate
1/2 cup paraffin
24 pecan halves

Combine the confectioners' sugar, butter, cream and vanilla in a large bowl and mix well to blend. Chill, covered, in the refrigerator or freezer.

Melt the chocolate and paraffin in a double boiler over hot water. Remove from the heat. Shape the chilled mixture into 24 small balls and dip into the chocolate mixture using a wooden pick. Drop onto waxed paper and top with a pecan half. Let stand until cool and set.

Makes 2 dozen

Louisiana Pralines

2 cups sugar
1/3 cup evaporated milk
1/2 cup light corn syrup

1/8 teaspoon baking soda
2 cups pecans
2 tablespoons butter

Combine the sugar, evaporated milk, corn syrup, baking soda and pecans in a heavy saucepan. Cook over medium heat to 234 to 240 degrees on a candy thermometer, soft-ball stage, stirring constantly. Add the butter and beat until the candy has a glossy appearance. Drop by teaspoonfuls onto waxed paper and let cool until set.

Makes 2 dozen

Traditional Toffee

2 cups (4 sticks) salted butter
1 tablespoon vinegar
2 cups sugar
1/2 cup pecans, finely chopped

12 (1.4-ounce) chocolate
candy bars
2 cups pecans, finely chopped

Melt the butter with the vinegar in a heavy 3-quart saucepan. Add the sugar and 1/2 cup pecans. Boil over medium heat to 300 degrees on a candy thermometer, hard-ball stage, stirring constantly. (The candy will burn very easily. The candy will become darker with streaks as the candy reaches 300 degrees.) Pour onto two or three buttered baking sheets, spreading thin. Melt the chocolate bars in a double boiler over hot water. Stir and spread thin over the toffee layers. Spread 2 cups pecans over the warm chocolate and press with the palms of your hands. Let stand until cool. Break into bite-size pieces and store in an airtight container. (Note: If you wish to coat both sides of the toffee with chocolate and pecans, double the amount of chocolate and pecans used and remove the toffee to buttered waxed paper after cooling slightly.)

Makes 6 dozen pieces

Barefoot Cookies

4 cups all-purpose flour, sifted
4 teaspoons baking powder
1 teaspoon ground cinnamon
1 (16-ounce) package brown sugar

1 1/2 cups shortening
2 eggs
2 cups pecans, chopped

Sift the flour, baking powder and cinnamon together. Cream the brown sugar and shortening in a mixing bowl until light and fluffy. Add the eggs one at a time, beating well after each addition. Stir in the flour mixture. Add the pecans and stir to mix well. Roll the dough into a log 1 1/2 inches in diameter. Wrap in waxed paper and chill for 4 hours. Unwrap the log and cut into thin slices. Place on a nonstick cookie sheet and bake at 300 degrees for 10 minutes. Remove to wire racks to cool.

Makes 5 to 6 dozen

German Chocolate Brownies

1 (2-layer) package German
  chocolate cake mix
3/4 cup (1 1/2 sticks)
  margarine, melted

1/3 cup evaporated milk
1 (14-ounce) package caramels
1/3 cup evaporated milk
2 cups (12 ounces) chocolate chips

Combine the cake mix, margarine and 1/3 cup evaporated milk in a bowl and mix well. Press one-half of the mixture into a greased and floured 9×13-inch baking pan. Bake at 350 degrees for 6 minutes.

Unwrap the caramels and place in a saucepan with 1/3 cup evaporated milk. Heat until the caramels melt, stirring constantly. Pour the caramel sauce over the baked layer and sprinkle with the chocolate chips. Spread the top with the remaining chocolate mixture and bake for 18 minutes.

Serves 12

Peppermint Brownies

BROWNIES

2 squares unsweetened chocolate

1/2 cup (1 stick) butter

2 eggs

1 cup sugar

1/2 cup sifted all-purpose flour

1/4 teaspoon salt

1/4 teaspoon peppermint extract

PEPPERMINT FROSTING

2 tablespoons butter, melted

1 cup confectioners' sugar

1 tablespoon cream

3/4 teaspoon peppermint extract

GERMAN CHOCOLATE FROSTING

2 tablespoons butter

6 squares German's sweet chocolate

To prepare the brownies, melt the chocolate and butter in a small saucepan over low heat, stirring constantly. Remove from the heat to cool. Beat the eggs in a mixing bowl until well beaten. Stir in the sugar, flour, salt and peppermint extract. Add the cooled chocolate mixture and mix well. Pour into a greased 8×8-inch baking pan. Bake at 350 degrees for 20 to 25 minutes or until the brownies pull away from the sides of the pan. Cool in the pan on a wire rack.

To prepare the peppermint frosting, combine the butter, confectioners' sugar and cream in a bowl and mix until smooth. Stir in the peppermint extract. Spread over the cooled brownies.

To prepare the chocolate frosting, melt the butter and chocolate in a saucepan over low heat, stirring constantly. Pour over the peppermint frosting, tilting the pan to cover. Chill for 1 hour before serving. (Note: You may double the recipe and bake in a 9×13-inch baking pan.)

Serves 9

DESSERT DIP

Soften 8 ounces cream cheese and 1/2 cup (1 stick) margarine. Beat the cream cheese and margarine in a mixing bowl until smooth and creamy. Add 3/4 cup confectioners' sugar, 2 tablespoons brown sugar and 1/2 teaspoon vanilla extract and beat well. Stir in one 10-ounce package miniature chocolate chips. Serve with chocolate graham crackers or animal crackers. Makes 2 cups.

Butterscotch Bars

BARS

1 cup (6 ounces) butterscotch chips
1/4 cup (1/2 stick) butter
3/4 cup all-purpose flour
1 teaspoon baking powder
3/4 teaspoon salt
2 eggs
1/2 teaspoon vanilla extract
1 cup packed brown sugar
1 cup (6 ounces) semisweet
   chocolate chips
3/4 cup chopped walnuts

BUTTERSCOTCH ICING
   (OPTIONAL)

1 tablespoon butter, softened
2 tablespoons brown sugar
1 tablespoon milk
1/2 cup confectioners' sugar

To prepare the bars, combine the butterscotch chips and butter in a microwave-safe bowl. Microwave on High at 30-second intervals, stirring after each interval until melted and smooth. Let stand until cool. Mix the flour, baking powder and salt together. Beat the eggs and vanilla in a large mixing bowl until well blended. Add the butterscotch mixture and mix well. Stir in the flour mixture until evenly mixed. Add the brown sugar, chocolate chips and walnuts and mix until combined. Spread the batter evenly in a greased 9×13-inch baking pan. Bake at 325 degrees for 30 minutes or until the bars just begin to pull away from the sides of the pan. Remove from the oven and cool completely.

To prepare the icing, heat the butter, brown sugar and milk in a small saucepan over medium-high heat until the brown sugar is well absorbed, stirring constantly. Remove from the heat to cool. Beat in the confectioners' sugar until smooth, adding additional milk or confectioners' sugar if needed for the desired consistency. Drizzle over the cooled bars. Let stand until set before cutting into bars.

Makes 18 bars

Carmelitas

1 (12-ounce) jar caramel sauce
4 1/2 tablespoons all-purpose flour
1 1/2 cups quick-cooking oats
1 1/2 cups all-purpose flour
1 1/4 cups packed brown sugar
3/4 teaspoon baking soda

1/3 teaspoon salt
1 1/4 cups (2 1/2 sticks) butter, melted
1 1/2 cups (9 ounces) chocolate chips
1 1/2 cups pecans, chopped

Mix the caramel sauce and 4 1/2 tablespoons flour in a bowl and set aside. Combine the oats, 1 1/2 cups flour, the brown sugar, baking soda, salt and melted butter in a bowl and stir to mix well. Press one-half of the oat mixture into a 9×11-inch baking pan coated with nonstick cooking spray. Bake at 350 degrees for 10 minutes. Remove from the oven and sprinkle with the chocolate chips. Pour the caramel mixture over the chocolate chips. Cover with the pecans and sprinkle with the remaining oat mixture. Return to the oven and bake for 20 minutes. Let cool and cut into squares.

Makes 40 squares

Chocolate Candy Crinkletops

2 cups all-purpose flour
2 teaspoons baking powder
2 cups sugar
1/2 cup (1 stick) butter
4 squares unsweetened baking chocolate, chopped

4 eggs, lightly beaten
2 teaspoons vanilla extract
1 1/2 cups chocolate candy miniature baking bits
1 cup sugar

Mix the flour and baking powder together. Combine 2 cups sugar, the butter and unsweetened baking chocolate in a 2-quart saucepan. Cook over medium heat until the butter and chocolate are melted, stirring constantly. Remove from the heat. Stir in the eggs and vanilla gradually. Add the flour mixture and mix until blended. Chill for 1 hour. Stir in the chocolate candy bits and chill for 1 hour.

Cover a small plate with 1 cup sugar. Shape the cookie dough into 1-inch balls using a melon baller or cookie scoop and roll in the sugar. Place 2 inches apart on foil-lined cookie sheets. Bake at 350 degrees for 10 to 12 minutes or until set. Do not overbake. Remove to wire racks to cool. Store in a tightly covered container.

Makes 5 dozen

Sugar and Spice Oatmeal Cookies

3/4 cup all-purpose flour
1/2 teaspoon baking soda
1/4 teaspoon salt
1/4 teaspoon pumpkin pie spice
1/2 cup (1 stick) butter, softened
1/2 cup granulated sugar
1/2 cup packed light brown sugar

1 egg
1/2 teaspoon vanilla extract
1 1/2 cups rolled oats
1/2 cup raisins
1/2 cup walnuts, chopped
2 tablespoons cinnamon-sugar

Mix the flour, baking soda, salt and pumpkin pie spice together. Beat the butter, granulated sugar and brown sugar in a mixing bowl until light and fluffy. Beat in the egg and vanilla. Add the flour mixture gradually, stirring well after each addition. Stir in the oats, raisins and walnuts. Drop by rounded teaspoonfuls onto greased cookie sheets. Flatten with a cup dipped in the cinnamon-sugar. Bake at 350 degrees for 8 to 10 minutes or until medium brown. Remove to wire racks to cool.

Makes 4 dozen

Ranger Cookies

5 cups rolled oats, finely ground
4 cups all-purpose flour
2 teaspoons baking powder
2 teaspoons baking soda
1 teaspoon salt
2 cups (4 sticks) butter, softened
2 cups granulated sugar
2 cups packed brown sugar
4 eggs

2 teaspoons vanilla extract
2 cups (12 ounces) chocolate chips
1 cup (6 ounces) butterscotch chips
1 cup (6 ounces) peanut
    butter chips
1 (8-ounce) chocolate candy
    bar, grated
3 cups ground walnuts

Mix the ground oats, flour, baking powder, baking soda and salt together. Cream the butter, granulated sugar and brown sugar in the mixing bowl of a stand mixer until light and fluffy. Add the eggs one at a time, beating well after each addition. Beat in the vanilla and oat mixture. Stir in the chocolate chips, butterscotch chips, peanut butter chips, candy bar and walnuts. Shape into balls using a medium cookie scoop and place 2 inches apart on ungreased cookie sheets. Bake at 375 degrees for 7 to 8 minutes or until golden brown. Remove to wire racks to cool. (Note: For a smaller batch, divide the ingredients by half.)

Makes 9 dozen

Apple Pie Deluxe

4 or 5 Granny Smith apples,
  peeled, cored and sliced
2/3 cup granulated sugar
1/3 cup packed brown sugar
2/3 teaspoon ground cinnamon
1/4 teaspoon ground allspice
  (optional)

1 tablespoon all-purpose flour
1/2 teaspoon salt
1/4 cup corn syrup
2 refrigerator pie pastries
1/2 cup (1 stick) butter
Cinnamon-sugar to taste

Combine the apples, granulated sugar, brown sugar, cinnamon, allspice, flour, salt and corn syrup in a large bowl and mix well. Line the bottom of a 9-inch pie plate with one of the pie pastries. Fill with the apple mixture. Cut the butter into small pieces and lay on top of the apple mixture. Place the remaining pie pastry on top, sealing the edge and cutting vents. Sprinkle with the cinnamon-sugar. Bake at 350 degrees for 30 to 40 minutes or until the top is golden brown.

Serves 8

Tart Cherry Pie

1 1/4 cups sugar
3 tablespoons cornstarch
1 teaspoon ground cinnamon
2 (14-ounce) cans tart red pie cherries
2 refrigerator pie pastries
Cinnamon-sugar

Combine the sugar, cornstarch and cinnamon in a bowl and mix well. Add the cherries and toss gently until coated. Let stand for 15 minutes or until syrupy. Line a 9-inch pie plate with one of the pie pastries. Fill with the cherry mixture. Top with the remaining pie pastry, sealing the edge and cutting vents. Sprinkle with cinnamon-sugar. Cover the edge of the pastry with foil and bake at 375 degrees for 30 minutes. Remove the foil and bake for 25 to 30 minutes longer or until golden brown.

Serves 6 to 8

Coconut Cream Pie

1 3/4 cups milk
1/2 cup sugar
1/2 teaspoon salt
3 1/2 tablespoons all-purpose flour
2 tablespoons cornstarch
1 egg plus 2 egg yolks, beaten
2 tablespoons butter
1/2 teaspoon vanilla extract

1/4 teaspoon almond extract
2 egg whites, at room temperature
1/4 cup sugar
3/4 cup grated flaked coconut
1 baked (10-inch) pie shell
1 cup heavy whipping
   cream, chilled
Vanilla extract to taste

Scald half the milk in a saucepan. Add 1/2 cup sugar and the salt. Bring to a slow boil, stirring frequently. Combine the flour, cornstarch and eggs in a bowl and mix well. Add the remaining milk and beat until smooth. Add a little of the scalded milk mixture and blend well. Combine with the remaining scalded milk mixture in a double boiler. Cook over hot water until thickened, stirring frequently. Remove from the heat. Add the butter, 1/2 teaspoon vanilla and the almond extract and beat until smooth. Cool slightly.

Beat the egg whites in a mixing bowl until frothy. Add 1/4 cup sugar gradually, beating until stiff peaks form. Fold about 1/4 cup of the custard into the egg whites and beat to mix thoroughly. Fold the remaining custard gently into the egg whites. Pulse the coconut in a food processor three or four times until finely ground. Fold 1/4 cup of the coconut into the custard mixture gently. Pour into the pie shell.

Whip the whipping cream and vanilla in a mixing bowl until soft peaks form. Spread over the top of the pie. Sprinkle with the remaining coconut and chill.

Serves 8

Chocolate Chip Pecan Pie

3 extra-large eggs
1 cup sugar
1 cup light corn syrup
3 tablespoons butter, melted
1 teaspoon vanilla extract
1/4 teaspoon salt
2 cups pecan halves
1/2 cup (3 ounces) semisweet chocolate chips
1 tablespoon bourbon
1 unbaked (9-inch) pie shell

Beat the eggs at low speed in a mixing bowl until light and fluffy. Stir in the sugar, corn syrup, melted butter, vanilla and salt with a spoon until blended. Stir in the pecan halves, chocolate chips and bourbon. Pour into the pie shell. Bake at 375 degrees for 55 to 60 minutes or until the center is set. Cool on a wire rack. Store any remaining pie in the refrigerator.

Serves 8

NEVER-FAIL PIECRUST

Mix 3 cups all-purpose flour and 1 teaspoon salt in a large bowl. Cut in 1 1/4 cups shortening until crumbly. Beat 1 egg, 5 tablespoons water and 1 tablespoon white vinegar in a mixing bowl until blended. Pour into the flour mixture all at once and blend with a spoon until moistened. Chill the pastry for a few minutes before rolling and fitting into pie plates. Makes enough pastry for 4 piecrusts.

Pumpkin Praline Pie with Chocolate Kahlúa Sauce

PIE
1 refrigerator pie pastry
6 tablespoons unsalted butter
$1/3$ cup packed brown sugar
$1/2$ cup chopped walnuts
3 egg yolks
$1^1/2$ cups eggnog
$1/2$ cup granulated sugar
2 envelopes unflavored gelatin
1 teaspoon ground cinnamon
$1/2$ teaspoon ground ginger
$1/2$ teaspoon ground nutmeg
Pinch of salt
2 cups pumpkin purée
3 egg whites, at room temperature
$1/4$ teaspoon cream of tartar

$1/4$ cup granulated sugar
1 cup heavy whipping
   cream, whipped

CHOCOLATE KAHLÚA SAUCE
$1/2$ cup heavy cream
3 tablespoons unsalted butter
$1/3$ cup granulated sugar
$1/3$ cup packed brown sugar
$1/8$ teaspoon salt
4 ounces semisweet chocolate, chopped
1 tablespoon Kahlúa

ASSEMBLY
Cinnamon to taste
Confectioners' sugar to taste

To prepare the pie, fit the pie pastry into a 9-inch pie plate, folding and fluting the edge. Prick the bottom and side of the pastry with a fork. Bake at 450 degrees for 10 minutes or until the edge is golden brown. Remove from the oven and maintain the oven temperature. Cream the butter and brown sugar in a mixing bowl until light and fluffy. Stir in the walnuts. Pour into the piecrust. Bake for 5 minutes. Remove from the oven to cool. Beat the egg yolks into the eggnog in a medium mixing bowl. Add $1/2$ cup granulated sugar, the gelatin, cinnamon, ginger, nutmeg and salt. Pour into a medium saucepan and heat slowly until the gelatin dissolves. Stir in the pumpkin. Pour into a large bowl and chill in the refrigerator. Beat the egg whites and cream of tartar in a mixing bowl until soft peaks form. Beat in $1/4$ cup granulated sugar until stiff. Fold the beaten egg whites and whipped cream into the pumpkin mixture. Spoon into the piecrust and chill for several hours before serving.

To prepare the sauce, combine the cream and butter in a heavy saucepan. Heat over medium heat until the butter melts but the cream is not boiling. Add the granulated sugar and brown sugar. Heat until dissolved, stirring constantly. Remove from the heat and add the salt and chocolate. Stir until the chocolate melts and the mixture is smooth. Stir in the Kahlúa.

To assemble, sprinkle cinnamon over each plate. Sprinkle with confectioners' sugar. Cut the pie into wedges and place a wedge in the center of each prepared plate. Drizzle the warm sauce over each piece of pie.

Serves 6 to 8

Caramel Nut Tart

SEMOLINA TART SHELL

2 cups all-purpose flour

1/2 cup semolina flour

1 teaspoon sugar

1/2 teaspoon salt

1/2 cup (1 stick) butter, chilled
   and cut into pieces

1/4 cup cold water

1/4 cup sour cream

TART

1 cup almonds

1 cup walnuts

1 cup hazelnuts

2 cups sugar

1 tablespoon light corn syrup

3/4 cup water

Pinch of salt

1 cup heavy cream

4 ounces dark chocolate, chopped

To prepare the tart shell, process the all-purpose flour, semolina flour, sugar, salt and butter in a food processor until the mixture resembles coarse cornmeal. Blend the cold water and sour cream together in a bowl. Add to the flour mixture, processing constantly for a few seconds until most of the liquid is absorbed. Shape the dough into a ball and wrap in plastic wrap. Chill in the refrigerator for 1 hour. Roll the dough into a 1/4-inch-thick circle on a lightly floured surface. Line a 10-inch tart pan with the pastry. Line the pastry with baking parchment or foil and fill with pie weights or dried beans. Bake at 350 degrees for 15 to 20 minutes or until light golden brown. Remove the baking parchment and pie weights.

To prepare the tart, spread the almonds, walnuts and hazelnuts in separate baking pans. Bake at 350 degrees until toasted and light golden brown. Maintain the oven temperature. Chop the almonds, walnuts and hazelnuts. Mix the nuts together and place in the baked tart shell. Combine the sugar, corn syrup and water in a saucepan. Heat over medium heat until the mixture turns a dark caramel color, swirling the mixture in the pan if the heat is uneven and part of the mixture begins to change color before the rest of it. Remove from the heat and whisk in the salt and 1/2 cup of the heavy cream. (Be careful, as the hot mixture will splatter as the cream is added.) Pour over the nut mixture and use a skewer or knife to distribute the caramel to the edge of the crust and spread out the nuts. Bake for 15 minutes or until bubbly on top. Remove from the oven and cool to room temperature. Remove the tart from the pan to a serving plate. Bring the remaining 1/2 cup cream to a simmer in a saucepan. Remove from the heat and whisk in the chocolate until smooth. Pour over the cooled tart. Chill for at least 1 hour before serving.

Serves 12

Apple Dumplings

2 Granny Smith apples,
   peeled and cored
2 (8-count) cans crescent
   roll dough
1 1/4 cups sugar

1/4 cup all-purpose flour
2 teaspoons ground cinnamon
3/4 cup (1 1/2 sticks)
   butter, melted
1 (12-ounce) can Sprite

Cut each apple into 8 slices. Unroll the crescent roll dough and separate into triangles. Place an apple slice on the wide end of each triangle and roll up. Place in a 9×13-inch baking pan. Mix the sugar, flour and cinnamon together. Add to the melted butter in a bowl and mix well. Spoon over the apple roll-ups. Pour the Sprite over the top. Bake at 350 degrees for 30 to 40 minutes or until brown.

Makes 16 dumplings

Creamy Banana Pudding

1 (6-ounce) package French
   vanilla instant pudding mix
1 1/2 cups milk
1 (14-ounce) can sweetened
   condensed milk

2 cups heavy whipping cream,
   whipped
3 bananas
Lemon juice
2 packages chessmen cookies or
   shortbread cookies

Whisk the pudding mix into the milk in a large bowl until smooth. Add the condensed milk and beat well. Chill for 5 minutes. Fold in the whipped cream.

Cut the bananas into slices and dip into lemon juice to prevent browning. Spoon 1 cup of the pudding mixture into a 2 1/2-quart glass serving bowl. Layer the cookies, bananas and remaining pudding mixture one-third at a time in the prepared dish, ending with the pudding mixture. Cover and chill in the refrigerator. Garnish as desired. Store in the refrigerator.

Serves 8 to 10

Bread Pudding

PUDDING

6 to 8 cups dry bread, crumbled

$2^1/2$ cups sugar

1 teaspoon ground cinnamon

1 teaspoon ground nutmeg

1 cup (2 sticks) butter, melted

4 cups half-and-half

6 eggs

2 egg whites

2 tablespoons vanilla extract

WHISKEY SAUCE

1 cup (2 sticks) butter, softened

3 cups confectioners' sugar

4 egg yolks

$1/4$ cup bourbon

$1/4$ cup water

To prepare the pudding, place the crumbled bread in a bowl and let stand, uncovered, at room temperature for 8 to 10 hours. Mix the sugar, cinnamon and nutmeg together. Pour over the crumbled bread and mix well. Add the melted butter and toss to coat. Combine 2 cups of the half-and-half, the eggs, egg whites and vanilla in a bowl and blend well. Pour over the bread mixture and mix well with clean hands. Add enough of the remaining half-and-half to make of a wet but not soupy consistency. Spoon into a baking dish. Bake at 350 degrees for 1 hour or until the top is golden brown.

To prepare the sauce, cream the butter and confectioners' sugar in a saucepan over medium heat until all the butter is absorbed. (Be careful not to caramelize the confectioners' sugar, as it will crystallize and the sauce will not be smooth.) Remove from the heat and blend in the egg yolks. Stir in the bourbon and water. Serve over the warm bread pudding.

Serves 16 to 20

SHORTBREAD

Mix 1 cup plus 3 tablespoons unbleached all-purpose flour and $1/3$ cup cornstarch together. Beat 10 tablespoons unsalted butter, softened, $1/4$ cup confectioners' sugar, $1^1/3$ tablespoons granulated sugar and $1/4$ teaspoon salt in a mixing bowl until fluffy. Sift the flour mixture gradually into the creamed mixture, beating constantly after each addition. Press the dough firmly into an 8×8-inch baking pan until smooth. Pierce the dough lightly with a fork into patterns of your choice. Bake at 300 degrees for 45 to 50 minutes or until the edges are slightly darker than the center. Remove the pan to a wire rack. Cool slightly and cut into the desired shapes. Makes 16 cookies.

Chocolate Crème Brûlée

3/4 cup granulated sugar
3 cups whipping cream
1 1/2 tablespoons chocolate liqueur
2 teaspoons vanilla extract

1/4 cup baking cocoa
1 ounce unsweetened chocolate
8 egg yolks, lightly beaten
1/2 cup packed brown sugar

Combine the granulated sugar, whipping cream, chocolate liqueur and vanilla in a heavy saucepan and stir to mix well. Cook over medium heat until the sugar melts and the mixture comes to a simmer, stirring constantly. Do not boil. Whisk in the baking cocoa and chocolate until blended. Remove from the heat. Beat the egg yolks in a large bowl. Add 1/4 cup of the warm cream mixture to the egg yolks gradually, stirring constantly. Stir in the remaining cream mixture. Pour into eight 4-ounce ramekins. Place the ramekins in a large roasting pan or two 9-inch baking pans. Add enough hot water to the roasting pan to come halfway up the sides of the ramekins. Bake at 350 degrees for 35 minutes. Remove the ramekins from the water and cool completely. Cover and chill until ready to serve.

To serve, place the ramekins on a baking sheet. Sprinkle the brown sugar evenly over the top of the custards. Broil 5 1/2 inches from the heat source for 3 minutes or until the brown sugar melts. Cool on wire racks until the brown sugar completely hardens.

Serves 8

Chocolate Pâte

6 tablespoons butter, cut into small pieces
2 3/4 cups chopped semisweet chocolate
3/4 cup whipping cream

Melt the butter and chocolate in a double boiler over hot water. Bring the whipping cream to a boil in a small saucepan. Pour over the chocolate mixture and stir until blended and smooth. Store, covered, in the refrigerator for up to 6 weeks. Use as a spread for shortbread for dessert. (Note: The chocolate mixture can be poured into any mold, such as a star, heart, tree, and so forth, to make serving more festive.)

Makes 2 3/4 cups

Lemon Velvet Ice Cream

1 1/4 cups fresh lemon juice
Zest of 2 lemons
4 cups sugar

1 quart milk
1 quart whipping cream
3 drops of yellow food coloring

Pour the lemon juice and lemon zest over the sugar in a saucepan and mix well. Let stand at room temperature for 1 hour. Heat the mixture until the sugar dissolves, stirring frequently. Remove from the heat. Stir in the milk, whipping cream and food coloring. Pour into an ice cream freezer container. Freeze using the manufacturer's directions.

Serves 20

Tutti Frutti Ice Cream

4 egg yolks
1 1/2 quarts half-and-half
2 cups sugar
3/4 cup mashed bananas
1/2 cup maraschino cherries, minced

3/4 cup strawberries, chopped
1 teaspoon vanilla extract
3/4 cup pecans, chopped
3 tablespoons fresh lemon juice
Pinch of salt

Whisk the egg yolks in a double boiler. Add the half-and-half and sugar and mix until the sugar is dissolved. Cook over boiling water for 5 minutes, stirring constantly. Remove from the heat to cool. Mix the bananas, cherries and strawberries in a bowl. Let stand for 5 minutes. Stir the vanilla into the cooled mixture. Add the fruit mixture and pecans and stir to mix well. Stir in the lemon juice and salt. Pour into an ice cream freezer container. Freeze using the manufacturer's directions.

Makes 1 gallon

CHOCOLATE SAUCE FOR ICE CREAM

Bring 6 tablespoons unsalted butter and 1/2 cup water to a boil in a saucepan. Add 3 ounces unsweetened chocolate. Heat until melted, stirring constantly. Add 1 cup sugar and 2 tablespoons light corn syrup. Boil gently for 5 minutes. Serve warm over ice cream. The sauce will harden and form a decadent shell when it hits the cold ice cream. Makes 2 cups.

Frozen Coffee Tiramisu

2/3 cup sugar
1/2 cup water
3/4 cup strong espresso
1/3 cup Kahlúa
2 quarts coffee ice cream
1 (3×7-inch) pound cake
8 ounces whipped topping
Toasted slivered almonds

Combine the sugar and water in a small saucepan and bring to a boil. Boil gently for 5 minutes or until slightly thickened, stirring occasionally. Remove from the heat and stir in the espresso. Let stand until lukewarm. Stir in the Kahlúa.

Remove 1 quart of the ice cream from the freezer and let stand until slightly softened. Cut the pound cake into 12 equal slices. Arrange one-half of the cake slices in a greased 8×8-inch flat dish. Spoon one-half of the espresso syrup over the cake slices. Beat the softened ice cream in a mixing bowl for a few seconds to soften enough to spread. Spread the ice cream evenly over the soaked cake. Cover with plastic wrap and freeze for 20 minutes.

Remove the remaining ice cream from the freezer and let stand until slightly softened. Remove the dish from the freezer. Arrange the remaining cake slices over the ice cream layer. Spoon the remaining espresso syrup over the cake slices. Spread the softened ice cream over the top. Cover the dish with plastic wrap and return to the freezer. Freeze for 2 hours or until firm. Remove from the freezer and spread with enough of the whipped topping to cover the top. Sprinkle with toasted almonds. Cover the dish with plastic wrap and freeze until firm. For ease of cutting, thaw for 10 minutes before serving. (Note: To make the strong espresso, use 3 heaping teaspoons of instant espresso crystals and 3/4 cup boiling water.)

Serves 9

Chocolate Trifle

1 (19-ounce) package fudge
   brownie mix
1/2 cup Kahlúa or other
   coffee-flavored liqueur

3 (4-ounce) packages chocolate
   instant pudding mix, prepared
12 ounces whipped topping
8 Heath candy bars, crushed

Prepare and bake the brownie mix using the package directions for a 9×13-inch baking pan. Prick the top of the warm brownies at 1-inch intervals using a fork. Drizzle with the Kahlúa and let cool. Crumble the brownies. Layer the brownies, pudding, whipped topping and candy one-third at a time in a trifle dish, ending with the candy. Chill for 8 hours before serving.

Serves 18

Strawberry Trifle

1 (14-ounce) can sweetened
   condensed milk
1 1/2 cups cold water
1 (4-ounce) package vanilla
   instant pudding mix
1 pint heavy whipping cream, chilled
1 teaspoon almond extract

3/4 cup strawberry preserves
   or jam
1/4 cup amaretto
1 (13-ounce) pound cake, cubed
2 quarts fresh strawberries, sliced
Strawberries
1/2 cup slivered almonds

Mix the condensed milk, water and pudding mix in a bowl. Chill for 5 minutes. Whip the whipping cream and almond extract in a mixing bowl until soft peaks form. Fold into the pudding mixture. Mix the preserves and amaretto in a bowl. Spread 2 cups of the pudding in a trifle bowl. Continue layering the cake cubes, sliced strawberries, preserve mixture and remaining pudding one-half at a time in the bowl. Garnish with strawberries and the almonds. Chill before serving.

Serves 18

STRAWBERRY PRESERVES

Rinse 5 cups of strawberries and remove the stems. Pour boiling water over the strawberries and drain at once. Boil the strawberries, 6 cups sugar and 2 tablespoons lemon juice in a saucepan for 10 minutes. Pour into flat containers and let stand for 24 hours to thicken, stirring frequently. Ladle into hot sterilized jars, leaving 1/2 inch headspace; seal with two-piece lids. Process in a boiling water bath for 10 minutes. Makes 32 ounces.

HELPFUL HINTS

Desserts

*I*cing will not become grainy if a pinch of salt is added to the sugar.

Frosting will look more professional if you first frost the cake with a thin layer and let it set before applying a second coating of frosting.

To freeze a frosted cake, place unwrapped in the freezer and freeze until firm. Then wrap the cake and return to the freezer. This prevents the frosting from sticking to the wrapping.

When you remove a cake from the oven, place the pan on a wet towel. This allows the cake to steam away from the sides and bottom of the pan, and it will come out easily in one piece.

To keep cakes moist, place half an apple in the cake box.

Unflavored, waxed dental floss is great for cutting iced cakes, like birthday cakes, and won't leave the icing a mess.

When measuring molasses, corn syrup, or other syrups, lightly butter the measuring cup first. Syrup will pour out nicely with no waste.

Dough won't stick to your hands if it is kneaded inside a large plastic bag.

When baking in a glass pan, reduce the oven temperature by 25 degrees.

For flakier piecrust, brush the top lightly with cold water before baking.

Empty plastic thread spools with slots on the ends can be pressed into sugar cookie dough to make interesting designs.

Create instant sorbets by freezing fruit juices in ice cube trays. When ready to use, pulse in a food processor until smooth.

You can usually substitute fruit juice in equal quantities for liqueur in a recipe without much change in taste.

Classic Cuisine

"*For the millions of us who live glued to computer keyboards at work and TV monitors at home, food may be more than entertainment. It may be the only sensual experience left.*"

—Barbara Ehrenreich

"*Food is not about impressing people. It's about making them feel comfortable.*"

—Ina Garten

"*As a child, my family's menu consisted of two choices: take it or leave it.*"

—Buddy Hackett

"*You can say this for ready-mixes: the next generation isn't going to have any trouble making pies exactly like Mother used to make.*"

—Earl Wilson

Parmesan Crisps

1 cup all-purpose flour
1/2 teaspoon baking powder
1/2 teaspoon salt
1/2 cup (1 stick) butter
1/2 cup (2 ounces) grated
    Parmesan cheese

2 tablespoons butter
1/4 cup (1 ounce) grated
    Parmesan cheese
2 tablespoons cream

Sift the flour, baking powder and salt together. Cream 1/2 cup butter in
a mixing bowl until soft. Add 1/2 cup Parmesan cheese and mix until blended.
Add the flour mixture and mix well. Roll into a thin circle on a lightly
floured surface. Cut into 1-inch circles. Place on a baking sheet and bake at
375 degrees for 8 to 10 minutes or until light brown. Cool on a wire rack.

Cream 2 tablespoons butter in a bowl until soft. Add 1/4 cup Parmesan cheese
and the cream and blend well. Spread one-half of the Parmesan crisps with the
cheese mixture and top with the remaining Parmesan crisps. (Note: If you don't
have a 1-inch cutter, use a vegetable oil cap. It is just the right size.)

Serves 8 to 10

Breakfast Gems

1 cup all-purpose flour
1/4 teaspoon salt
1/2 cup (1 stick) butter or
    margarine
3/4 cup sugar
3 eggs, at room temperature

2 teaspoons vanilla extract
1/2 cup sugar
1 teaspoon ground cinnamon
1/2 cup (1 stick) butter or
    margarine, melted

Sift the flour and salt together. Cream 1/2 cup butter in a mixing bowl until
soft. Add 3/4 cup sugar and beat until well blended. Add the eggs one at a
time, beating well after each addition. Add the vanilla and beat until the mixture
is light and fluffy. Stir in the flour mixture gently. Fill greased 21/2-inch
muffin cups two-thirds full. Bake at 350 degrees for 20 minutes. Cool in the
pan for 5 minutes. Mix 1/2 cup sugar and the cinnamon together. Quickly
dip each warm muffin in 1/2 cup melted butter and roll in the cinnamon-sugar.
(Note: You may bake in small muffin cups and bake for 10 to 15 minutes or
until the muffins test done.)

Makes 21/2 dozen

Roast Beef with Horseradish Sauce

BEEF

1 (4- to 8-pound) rolled rib roast
Salt and pepper to taste
Garlic salt to taste
Chopped onion to taste
1/2 cup water

HORSERADISH SAUCE

Sour cream
Horseradish
Chopped chives to taste
Worcestershire sauce to taste
Salt and pepper to taste

To prepare the beef, season the beef with salt, pepper and garlic salt. Place in a roasting pan and add some chopped onion and the water. Insert a meat thermometer into the center of the beef. Place in a 350-degree oven and reduce the oven temperature to 200 degrees. Bake the beef for about 1 hour per pound or to 145 degrees on a meat thermometer for medium-rare, 160 degrees for medium or 170 degrees for well done.

To prepare the sauce, mix equal parts of sour cream and horseradish in a bowl. Season with chives, Worcestershire sauce, salt and pepper. Serve with the sliced beef.

Serves 8 to 10

155

BEEF DIP

Soften 16 ounces cream cheese in a bowl. Add 2 cups sour cream, 1/4 cup milk, 1/4 cup minced green bell pepper, 1/4 cup minced onion, 8 ounces dried beef and 1/4 teaspoon pepper in a bowl and mix well. Spoon into a 1 1/2-quart baking dish. Bake at 350 degrees for 30 minutes. Sprinkle with 1/2 cup chopped nuts. Serve hot with assorted crackers. Makes 5 cups.

Lobster-Stuffed Beef Tenderloin

1 (3- to 4-pound) beef tenderloin
2 (8-ounce) frozen lobster tails
Salt to taste
2 tablespoons butter, melted
1 tablespoon lemon juice
6 slices bacon, partially cooked
1/2 cup sliced green onions
1/2 cup (1 stick) butter
1/2 to 3/4 cup dry white wine
3 garlic cloves, minced
Mushrooms
Sprigs of fresh parsley

Cut the beef lengthwise to but not through the bottom to butterfly. Cook the frozen lobster tails in boiling salted water to cover in a large saucepan. Return to a boil and reduce the heat. Simmer for 5 to 6 minutes or until the lobster meat is opaque. Remove the lobster from the shells and cut into halves lengthwise. Place the lobster end to end inside the beef. Mix 2 tablespoons melted butter and the lemon juice together and drizzle over the lobster. Wrap the beef around the lobster to enclose and tie together with string at 1-inch intervals. Place on a rack in a shallow roasting pan. Roast at 425 degrees for 45 to 50 minutes for rare. Lay the bacon slices on top of the beef and roast for 5 minutes.

Sauté the green onions in 1/2 cup butter in a saucepan until tender. Add the wine and garlic and sauté until heated through.

To serve, cut the roast into slices and place on a serving platter. Spoon the sauce over the roast and garnish with mushrooms and parsley.

Serves 8

Thin Veal Forestière

1 1/2 pounds thin veal cutlets
1 garlic clove
All-purpose flour
1/4 cup (1/2 stick) butter, melted
8 ounces mushrooms, thinly sliced

Salt and pepper to taste
1/2 cup dry vermouth
2 teaspoons lemon juice
Chopped parsley

Pound the veal very thin. Rub each cutlet with the garlic clove and dip into flour to coat well. Brown the cutlets in the melted butter in a skillet. Heap the mushrooms on top of the cutlets and season with salt and pepper. Add the vermouth. Cover and cook over low heat for 20 minutes or until the cutlets are fork-tender, adding water if needed to keep the cutlets moist. Sprinkle with the lemon juice and parsley just before serving.

Serves 4 to 6

Quiche Lorraine

1 unbaked (9-inch) pie shell
4 slices bacon, cooked and crumbled
8 paper-thin slices ham, shredded
8 paper-thin slices Swiss cheese
4 thin slices onion, sautéed
3 eggs

1/4 teaspoon salt
1 teaspoon chopped chives
1 teaspoon dry mustard
1 cup half-and-half, heated
Grated nutmeg to taste

Prick the bottom of the pie shell with a fork. Bake at 450 degrees for 10 minutes or until flaky but not brown. Reduce the oven temperature to 350 degrees. Sprinkle the bacon in the baked pie shell. Layer one-half of the ham, one-half of the Swiss cheese, the sautéed onion, remaining ham and remaining cheese over the bacon. Beat the eggs in a bowl until light. Add the salt, chives, dry mustard and hot half-and-half and beat well. Pour over the layers and let stand for 10 minutes. Sprinkle the top with nutmeg. Bake for 45 minutes or until set.

Serves 6

Hot Chicken Salad

2 to 3 cups chopped cooked chicken
2/3 cup chopped celery
1 (8-ounce) can water
   chestnuts, chopped
1/2 cup slivered almonds
1 (6-ounce) package frozen
   chopped onions

8 ounces Cheddar cheese, shredded
1 cup mayonnaise
Juice of 1 lemon
Poultry seasoning, paprika and
   MSG to taste
Crushed potato chips

Mix the chicken, celery, water chestnuts, almonds, onions, Cheddar cheese, mayonnaise, lemon juice, poultry seasoning, paprika and MSG in a large bowl. Spoon into a 9×13-inch baking dish. Chill, covered, for 8 to 10 hours. Uncover and top the chicken mixture with crushed potato chips. Bake at 450 degrees for 12 to 15 minutes or until brown and bubbly. (Note: For presentation, serve the chicken salad in individual pastry shells or ramekins—perfect for an afternoon get-together.)

Serves 6 to 8

Rock Cornish Game Hens Continental

4 Rock Cornish game hens
Salt, pepper and paprika to taste
1/2 cup (1 stick) butter
2 onions, finely chopped

1 cup brandy
2 tablespoons all-purpose flour
2 cups sour cream

Split the hens into halves and sprinkle both sides with salt, pepper and paprika. Melt the butter in a large skillet and add the onions. Add the hens and sauté gently over medium heat for 5 minutes or until brown on both sides. Add the brandy. Cover and simmer for 10 minutes or until the hens are tender. Remove the hens to a warm platter. Blend the flour into the pan drippings. Cook over medium heat until thickened, stirring constantly. Blend in the sour cream. Cook just until heated through; do not boil. Serve with the hens.

Serves 8

Hot Seafood Salad

1 large green bell pepper, finely chopped
1 large onion, finely chopped
1 cup finely chopped celery
1 cup peeled cooked shrimp
1 cup cooked crab meat
1 cup mayonnaise
1 teaspoon salt
1 teaspoon pepper
1 teaspoon Worcestershire sauce
Cracker crumbs

Cook the bell pepper, onion and celery in a small amount of water in a saucepan until tender; drain. Combine with the shrimp, crab meat, mayonnaise, salt, pepper and Worcestershire sauce in a bowl and mix well. Spoon into a baking dish or individual shells. Top with cracker crumbs. Bake at 300 degrees for 20 to 30 minutes or until brown and bubbly.

Serves 6

PARTY SANGRIA

Combine 1 1/2 bottles zinfandel, 2 cups orange juice, 2 cups soda water, 1 cup lemon juice, 3 tablespoons brandy, 2 tablespoons Strega and 1/4 cup sugar in a large pitcher and stir until the sugar is dissolved. Add 6 thin slices orange, cut into halves, 4 thin slices lemon, cut into quarters, and 3 peaches, peeled and sliced. Serve very cold with fruit garnish in each glass. Serves 6.

Seafood au Gratin

Handful of salt
1 cup cider vinegar
5 pounds frozen lobster tails
   (3^1/2 pounds after cleaning)
Handful of salt
1 cup cider vinegar
5 pounds shrimp
   (3^1/2 pounds after cleaning)
1 cup (2 sticks) butter
1 cup all-purpose flour
7 cups milk
1 cup tomato purée

1^2/3 tablespoons salt
^{1}/2 teaspoon cayenne pepper
1^1/2 teaspoons paprika
2 garlic cloves, minced
2 tablespoons MSG
5 ounces Gruyère cheese,
   cut into small pieces
4 ounces American cheese,
   cut into small pieces
2 pounds crab meat
^{1}/2 cup sherry (optional)
5 cups hot cooked rice

Bring water, a handful of salt and 1 cup cider vinegar to a boil in a large stockpot. Plunge the lobster tails into the water. Cover and cook over high heat for 20 minutes. Drain and cool. Slit the shells and remove the lobster meat. Remove the dark vein from the center of the tail meat. Cut the lobster meat into bite-size pieces.

Bring water, a handful of salt and 1 cup cider vinegar to a boil in a large stockpot. Add the shrimp. Cover and cook over high heat for 10 minutes or until the shrimp turn pink. Peel and devein the shrimp.

Melt the butter in a large saucepan and stir in the flour until blended. Cook over low heat for 1 minute, stirring constantly. Add the milk, tomato purée, 1^2/3 tablespoons salt, the cayenne pepper, paprika, garlic, MSG, Gruyère cheese and American cheese. Cook over low heat until the cheeses have melted and the sauce is thick and bubbly.

To serve, heat the sauce in a double boiler about 2 hours before serving. Mix the lobster, shrimp, crab meat, wine and sauce together about 1 hour before serving. Serve over the rice.

Serves 20

Gilded Green Beans

GREEN BEANS

6 tablespoons vinegar

3/4 cup vegetable oil or olive oil

2 onions, minced

Salt and pepper to taste

2 pounds cooked whole green beans

8 slices bacon, crisp-cooked
    and crumbled

DRESSING

8 hard-cooked eggs, chopped

6 tablespoons mayonnaise

4 teaspoons vinegar

2 teaspoons prepared mustard

Salt to taste

To prepare the green beans, mix the vinegar, oil, onions, salt and pepper in a bowl. Place the green beans in a shallow dish and pour the marinade over the top. Chill, covered, for several hours. Drain the green beans, discarding the marinade. Toss the green beans with the bacon and place in a serving bowl.

To prepare the dressing, combine the eggs, mayonnaise, vinegar, mustard and salt in a bowl and mix well. Pour the dressing over the green beans. (Note: You may serve as individual salads on lettuce leaves or as a cold vegetable dish.)

Serves 8

Country Club Onions

6 large Bermuda onions, thinly
    sliced and separated into rings

2 cups water

8 ice cubes

1/2 cup vinegar

1 tablespoon sugar

1 teaspoon salt

1/2 cup mayonnaise

1 to 2 tablespoons celery seeds

Combine the onion rings, water, ice cubes, vinegar, sugar and salt in a large container. Cover and chill for 2 to 10 hours. Remove the onion rings to paper towels to drain, discarding the marinade. Place the onion rings in a large bowl. Combine the mayonnaise and celery seeds in a small bowl and mix well. Add to the onion rings and toss to coat.

Serves 20

New Potatoes with Caper Sauce

12 small new potatoes
1/2 cup (1 stick) butter
1/4 cup (1 ounce) grated
    Parmesan cheese
2 tablespoons grated onion

2 tablespoons chopped parsley
2 tablespoons chopped capers
1 teaspoon caper juice
1/4 teaspoon pepper
1/2 teaspoon salt, or to taste

Cook the potatoes in water to cover in a saucepan until tender; drain. Melt the butter in a small saucepan. Stir in the Parmesan cheese, onion, parsley, capers, caper juice and pepper. Cook over low heat until blended, stirring constantly. Season with the salt. Place the potatoes in a serving bowl. Add the sauce and toss until the potatoes are well coated. Serve immediately. (Note: This sauce is also good served on other vegetables, such as carrots and peas.)

Serves 4 to 6

Golden Potato Casserole

6 potatoes
1/2 cup (1 stick) butter
2 cups (8 ounces) shredded
    Cheddar cheese
2 cups sour cream

1/3 cup chopped green
    onions with tops
1 teaspoon salt
1/4 teaspoon pepper
2 tablespoons butter

Boil the unpeeled potatoes in water to cover in a saucepan until tender. Drain and peel the potatoes. Grate the potatoes and place in a bowl. Combine 1/2 cup butter and the Cheddar cheese in a saucepan and heat until almost melted, stirring constantly. Chill in the refrigerator. Blend the sour cream, green onions, salt and pepper into the cheese mixture. Pour over the potatoes and stir in lightly. Spoon into a 2-quart baking dish and dot with 2 tablespoons butter. Bake at 350 degrees for 40 minutes.

Serves 10 to 12

Yam Soufflé

3 pounds yams
1 cup (2 sticks) butter, melted
1 1/2 cups confectioners' sugar
1/2 teaspoon grated nutmeg
Dash of ground cloves

1 1/2 teaspoons grated lemon zest
2 tablespoons brandy
6 egg yolks
6 egg whites, stiffly beaten

Boil the unpeeled yams in water to cover in a large saucepan until tender. Drain and peel the yams. Mash the yams in a mixing bowl. Stir in the melted butter, confectioners' sugar, nutmeg, cloves, lemon zest, brandy and egg yolks. Cool slightly. Fold in the stiffly beaten egg whites. Spoon into a greased 1 1/2-quart baking dish. Bake at 325 degrees for 1 hour.

Serves 8 to 10

Oatmeal Cake

CAKE
1 1/4 cups boiling water
1 cup rolled oats
1 1/3 cups all-purpose flour
1 teaspoon baking soda
1/2 teaspoon salt
1/2 teaspoon ground cinnamon
1/2 cup (1 stick) butter, softened
1 cup packed brown sugar
1 cup granulated sugar

2 eggs
1 teaspoon vanilla extract

NUTTY COCONUT TOPPING
6 tablespoons butter, softened
1/2 cup packed brown sugar
1/4 cup milk
1 teaspoon vanilla extract
1 cup grated coconut
1 cup chopped nuts

To prepare the cake, pour the boiling water over the oats in a bowl and let stand for 20 minutes. Mix the flour, baking soda, salt and cinnamon together. Cream the butter, brown sugar and granulated sugar in a mixing bowl until light and fluffy. Add the eggs and beat well. Add the flour mixture gradually, beating constantly after each addition. Stir in the oatmeal and vanilla. Pour into a greased 8×10-inch cake pan and bake at 350 degrees for 40 minutes. Cool in the pan for 5 to 10 minutes.

To prepare the topping, cream the butter and brown sugar in a mixing bowl until light and fluffy. Add the milk and vanilla and mix well. Stir in the coconut and nuts. Spread over the warm cake. Broil for a few minutes or until light brown.

Serves 12

Peach Cobbler

¹/2 cup (1 stick) butter
4 peaches, peeled and sliced
1 cup sugar
1 recipe pie pastry, prepared

3 tablespoons butter, melted
3 tablespoons sugar (optional)
1 tablespoon ground cinnamon

Melt ¹/2 cup butter in a 9-inch pie pan and remove from the heat. Add the peaches and cover with 1 cup sugar. Roll the pastry on a lightly floured surface and cut into strips. Criss-cross the pastry strips over the top of the peaches. Brush the pastry with 3 tablespoons melted butter. Mix 3 tablespoons sugar and the cinnamon together and sprinkle over the top of the pie. Bake at 350 degrees for 50 to 60 minutes or until golden brown.

Serves 6

English Toffee Cookies

1 cup (2 sticks) butter, softened
1 cup packed brown sugar
1 egg yolk
2 cups all-purpose flour

1 teaspoon vanilla extract
1 egg white
¹/2 cup finely chopped pecans

Cream the butter and brown sugar in a mixing bowl until light and fluffy. Add the egg yolk, flour and vanilla and mix well. Spread in a greased 9×13-inch baking pan. Dip your fingertips in the unbeaten egg white and spread over the top to smooth the surface. (You will not need all of the egg white.) Sprinkle with the pecans and press in gently. Bake at 300 degrees for 40 to 45 minutes or until golden brown. Remove from the oven and immediately cut into squares.

Makes 2 dozen

POTATO CHIP COOKIES

Cream 2 cups butter, softened, and 1 cup granulated sugar in a mixing bowl until light and fluffy. Add 3 cups all-purpose flour and 2 teaspoons vanilla extract and mix well. Stir in 1¹/2 cups crushed potato chips. Drop by teaspoonfuls onto greased cookie sheets. Bake at 350 degrees for 12 to 15 minutes or until light golden brown. Remove to wire racks to cool. Sift confectioners' sugar onto all sides of the cooled cookies. Makes 8 dozen.

Classic Cuisine

Selections in the Classic Cuisine portion of this cookbook are a
tribute to the previous Junior League of Wichita Falls cookbooks,
Discoveries in Dining and *Home Cookin'*. These tried and true recipes are provided
by our sustaining members and are sure to become traditions in your home.
We hope you will find these recipes unique and quite possibly
the "best of the best." This collection from our past is as much a part of
the history of the Junior League of Wichita Falls as we hope our
newest cookbook will be for future generations.

International Flair

"*F*ood is our common ground, a universal experience."

—James Beard

"*F*ood is a central activity of mankind and one of the
single most significant trademarks of a culture."

—Mark Kurlansky

"*F*ood is so primal, so essential a part of our lives, often the mere
sharing of recipes with strangers turns them into good friends.
That's why I love this community."

—Jasmine Heiler

"*F*ood, to a large extent is what holds a society together, and eating
is closely linked to deep spiritual experiences."

—Peter Farb and George Armelagos

Pea Soup (Dutch)

3 cups dried green split peas
3 quarts water
2 large pork loin sirloin chops
1 pound bacon (in 1 piece)
2 beef bouillon cubes
3 leeks, sliced
1 onion, sliced
3 large carrots, sliced

3 celery ribs with green
    leaves, sliced
1 celery root or celeriac,
    cut into cubes
1 large potato, cut into cubes
1 smoked sausage link, sliced
Salt, pepper, Maggi seasoning and
    chopped parsley to taste

Sort and rinse the peas. Soak the peas in the water in a large stockpot for 30 minutes to soften. Add the pork chops, bacon and bouillon cubes. Bring to a boil and reduce the heat. Simmer for 1 hour. Add the leeks, onion, carrots, celery, celery root and potato and simmer for 1 hour or until soft. Remove the pork chops and bacon to a cutting board and cut into pieces. Return to the stockpot. Stir in the smoked sausage and seasonings. Ladle into soup bowls.

Serves 6 to 8

Designer Fudge (Dutch)

BASIC FUDGE
$1^1/3$ cups granulated sugar
1 cup packed light brown sugar
Pinch of salt
$3/4$ cup milk or half-and-half
1 tablespoon butter

FLAVORING OPTIONS
    (Select One)
$1/4$ cup brewed espresso
$1/4$ cup prepared cocoa
3 tablespoons whipping cream
2 tablespoons maraschino juice
2 teaspoons almond, lemon or
    orange extract

Combine the granulated sugar, brown sugar, salt, milk and butter in a heavy saucepan and mix well. (If you chose the flavoring option of the espresso, cocoa or whipping cream, add your choice at this point.) Bring the mixture to a boil, stirring constantly. Cook to 234 to 240 degrees on a candy thermometer, soft-ball stage, stirring constantly. Remove the pan from the heat. (If you chose the flavoring option of the maraschino juice or the almond, lemon or orange extract, add your choice at this point.) Pour the mixture directly onto a piece of foil with the edges raised to hold the mixture at the desired thickness, usually $1/3$ inch thick. Let cool for 1 hour. Cut into squares with a cold knife. Store in airtight containers lined with waxed paper, placing waxed paper between each layer as well.

Makes 1 pound

German Beef Stew (German)

2/3 pound beef chuck
2 tablespoons prepared mustard
1 tablespoon butter
1 tablespoon vegetable oil
1 teaspoon paprika
1/2 teaspoon salt
2 teaspoons all-purpose flour
2 onions
3 cups (or more) hot beef stock
1/2 cup dry sherry
1 bay leaf

2 small potatoes, peeled and cut
    into 1/3-inch cubes
2 mushrooms, thinly sliced
1/2 green bell pepper, seeded
    and chopped
1/2 red bell pepper, seeded
    and chopped
1 tablespoon ketchup
2 tablespoons red wine
Salt and freshly ground
    pepper to taste
Tabasco sauce to taste

Cut the beef into 1/2-inch cubes, removing all fat and skin. Mix the beef with the mustard in a bowl until all the pieces are coated. Sear the beef in the hot butter and oil in a heavy medium saucepan for 5 minutes or until brown. Season with 1 teaspoon paprika and 1/2 teaspoon salt. Add the flour and cook for 5 minutes or until the mixture is thick and dark brown, stirring constantly. Add the onions, beef stock, wine and bay leaf. Cover and return to a boil. Reduce the heat and simmer for 45 minutes, stirring occasionally. Add the potatoes, mushrooms and bell peppers. Simmer for 30 minutes, stirring occasionally. Stir in the ketchup and wine. Add additional beef stock if needed for the desired consistency. Season with salt, pepper and Tabasco sauce. Discard the bay leaf before serving.

Serves 4

Rouladen (German)

6 rouladen slices (top round or
    sirloin tip $1/8$ to $1/4$ inch thick)
Salt and freshly ground pepper
    to taste
10 to 12 teaspoons Dijon mustard
$2^3/4$ to 3 cups finely
    chopped onions

6 bacon slices, cut into small pieces
2 dill pickles, chopped (optional)
Vegetable oil
2 cups beef stock
$1/3$ cup red wine
$1/4$ to $1/3$ cup sour cream

Place the beef on a flat surface and sprinkle with salt and pepper. Spread each piece with $1^3/4$ to 2 teaspoons mustard. Sprinkle each piece with 3 to 4 tablespoons onions and one-sixth of the bacon. Top each with a small amount of chopped pickles. Roll up the beef to enclose the filling and tie each securely with string or wooden picks. Sauté the remaining onions in hot oil in a skillet until golden brown. Add the beef roll-ups and cook until brown on all sides. Add the beef stock and wine. Cover and braise gently for $1^1/2$ to 2 hours or until fork-tender. Remove the beef roll-ups from the skillet. Stir the sour cream into the pan drippings in the skillet. Cook for 3 to 5 minutes, stirring constantly. Return the beef roll-ups to the skillet. Cook until heated through.

Serves 4 to 6

Sauerkraut Goulash (German)

4 onions, finely chopped
5 tablespoons butter, melted
1 to $1^1/2$ pounds boneless lean
    pork, cut into medium cubes
1 pound sauerkraut, cut into
    small pieces

1 teaspoon paprika
$1/2$ teaspoon salt
$8^1/2$ ounces bouillon
$1/2$ cup sour cream
Salt to taste

Sauté the onions in the melted butter in a large saucepan until translucent. Add the pork and sauté for 2 to 3 minutes or until brown. Stir in the undrained sauerkraut, paprika and $1/2$ teaspoon salt. Stir in the bouillon. Cover and simmer over low heat for 1 hour. Drain the goulash, reserving the liquid in a bowl. Stir the sour cream into the reserved liquid. Pour the sour cream mixture over the goulash gradually, stirring constantly. Season with additional salt if needed. Cook until heated through. Serve immediately. (Note: Hot cooked rice is a great side dish for this goulash.)

Serves 4 to 6

Elegant Red Cabbage (German)

2 pounds red cabbage, thinly sliced
1 1/2 cups apple juice
1/2 cup merlot or other red wine
2 Jonagold, Gala or Braeburn
    apples, peeled and cut into
    small pieces
1 bay leaf
Salt to taste

2 tablespoons merlot or other
    red wine
1/4 cup honey
2 tablespoons water
1/2 teaspoon vanilla extract
Black pepper and cayenne pepper
    to taste

Combine the cabbage, apple juice, 1/2 cup wine, the apples, bay leaf and salt in a large saucepan. Cover and bring to a boil over medium-high heat. Reduce the heat and simmer for 45 minutes, stirring occasionally. Heat 2 tablespoons wine, the honey, water, vanilla, salt, black pepper and cayenne pepper in a small saucepan until combined, stirring constantly. Stir into the cabbage mixture. Cook for 10 minutes or until the cabbage is tender. Adjust the seasonings to taste. Remove the bay leaf before serving.

Serves 4

Fresh Fruit Kuchen (German)

1 cup cake flour, sifted
1/2 teaspoon baking powder
1/4 teaspoon salt
2/3 cup sugar
3/4 teaspoon grated lemon zest
1/4 cup plus 1 teaspoon butter

2 eggs, beaten
2 to 3 cups sliced apples
1 egg, beaten
3 tablespoons whipping cream
1/2 teaspoon ground cinnamon
Whipped cream

Sift the cake flour, baking powder, salt and 2 tablespoons of the sugar into a bowl. Add the lemon zest. Cut in the butter with a pastry blender until crumbly. Add 2 eggs and mix to form a soft dough. Press to form a thin layer over the bottom and up the sides of a greased 9×9-inch baking pan. Arrange the apples in the prepared pan. Beat 1 egg, the remaining sugar and whipping cream in a bowl. Pour over the apples. Sprinkle with the cinnamon. Bake at 375 degrees for 25 minutes or until the apples are tender. Serve with whipped cream.

Serves 8

Honey Puffs (Greek)

1 envelope dry yeast, or 1 ounce
  fresh yeast
2 cups warm water
1 teaspoon sugar
4 cups all-purpose flour

1 teaspoon salt
1 quart vegetable oil for frying
Honey
Ground cinnamon

Dissolve the yeast in 1 cup of the warm water in a large bowl. Add the sugar and 1 1/2 cups of the flour and beat until smooth. Cover and let rise in a warm place until doubled in bulk. Add the remaining 1 cup warm water, the salt and enough of the remaining flour to form a thick batter. Cover and let rise for 1 1/2 hours or until the mixture begins to bubble. Heat the oil in a deep fryer until the oil begins to smoke. Drop the dough by small spoonfuls (about ten at a time) into the hot oil. Deep-fry over medium-low heat until puffed and golden brown. Remove with a slotted spoon. Drizzle with honey and sprinkle with cinnamon. Serve hot.

Makes 6 dozen

Spinach Pie (Greek)

2 (10-ounce) packages chopped
  frozen spinach, thawed, drained
  and squeezed dry
4 eggs, lightly beaten
8 ounces crumbled feta cheese
1 large yellow onion, finely chopped
1 garlic clove, finely chopped

2 tablespoons olive oil
1/4 cup all-purpose flour
1 tablespoon finely chopped parsley
Salt and pepper to taste
1 pound phyllo dough
3/4 cup (1 1/2 sticks) butter, melted

Mix the spinach, eggs and feta cheese in a bowl. Sauté the onion and garlic in the olive oil in a skillet until brown. Add to the spinach mixture. Stir in the flour, parsley, salt and pepper. Layer 6 of the phyllo sheets in a buttered 9×12-inch baking dish, brushing the sheets with one-third of the melted butter. Keep the remaining phyllo dough covered with a moist kitchen towel to prevent drying out. Spread one-half of the spinach mixture evenly over the phyllo layers to within 1/2 inch of the edges. Layer 6 of the remaining phyllo sheets over the spinach mixture, brushing the sheets with one-half of the remaining melted butter. Spread the remaining spinach mixture over the phyllo layers. Layer the remaining phyllo dough over the top, brushing the sheets with the remaining butter. Cover and chill for 30 minutes. Bake at 350 degrees for 30 minutes or until set. Cool for 20 minutes and cut into squares. Serve at room temperature.

Serves 10 to 12

Stuffed Grape Leaves (Greek)

1 cup long grain white rice
1 cup finely chopped yellow onion
1 garlic clove, minced
1 cup plus 2 tablespoons olive oil
3 green onions with tops,
   finely chopped
1/4 cup fresh parsley, minced
1 tablespoon minced fresh mint
1/4 cup pine nuts
1 teaspoon ground cinnamon

1/2 teaspoon ground allspice
1/2 teaspoon salt
1/4 teaspoon freshly ground pepper
1 (16-ounce) jar grape leaves
Several sprigs of fresh parsley
3/4 cup fresh lemon juice
1 cup chicken broth, stock or
   water, heated
Fresh lemon juice to taste
Grated or minced lemon zest

Rinse the rice and drain. Sauté the onion and garlic in 3 tablespoons of the olive oil in a skillet over medium-high heat for 5 minutes or until soft but not brown. Spoon into a bowl. Add the rice, 1/2 cup of the olive oil, the green onions, minced parsley, mint, pine nuts, cinnamon, allspice, salt and pepper and mix well.

Rinse the grape leaves under cold running water to remove as much of the brine as possible. Pat dry and stack on a plate. Place 1 leaf shiny side down on a flat work surface. Cut off and discard the tough stem end. Spoon about 1 tablespoon of the rice mixture in the center near the base of the leaf. Fold the stem end over to cover the filling. Fold both sides inward lengthwise and tightly roll the leaf toward the pointed tip end to form a compact packet. Repeat with the remaining leaves and filling.

Pour 2 tablespoons of the remaining olive oil into a large stockpot, tilting to cover the bottom of the pan. Add a layer of parsley sprigs to prevent the grape leaves from sticking. Arrange the stuffed grape leaves seam side down and almost touching on top of the parsley, making as many layers as necessary.

Drizzle the remaining 5 tablespoons olive oil, 3/4 cup lemon juice and 1/2 cup heated chicken broth over the leaves. Top with a heat-resistant plate and weight with a heavy can to keep the leaves from unwinding during the cooking process. Cover the stockpot. Bring to a gentle boil and reduce the heat to low. Cook for 1 hour or until the rice is tender, adding the remaining chicken broth as needed to keep the grape leaves moist. Remove from the heat and cool in the stockpot. Sprinkle with lemon juice to taste and garnish with lemon zest. Serve at room temperature.

Serves 6 to 8

Baklava (Greek)

1 pound phyllo dough
3 cups finely chopped pecans
1/4 cup sugar
1 tablespoon ground cinnamon
Pinch of ground cloves
2 cups (4 sticks) butter, melted
2 cups sugar

1 cup water
Slice of lemon
Strip of orange rind
2 cinnamon sticks
1/4 cup honey
1/2 teaspoon vanilla extract

Let the phyllo dough thaw in the refrigerator for at least 6 hours before using. Mix the pecans, 1/4 cup sugar, the ground cinnamon and cloves in a bowl. Brush a 10×15-inch baking pan with some of the melted butter. Layer 7 or 8 sheets of the phyllo dough in the prepared pan, brushing the layers with one-third of the remaining butter. Sprinkle with one-half of the pecan mixture. Layer 7 to 8 sheets of the phyllo dough over the pecan mixture, brushing the layers with one-half of the remaining butter. Sprinkle with the remaining pecan mixture. Top with the remaining phyllo sheets, brushing the layers with the melted butter. Cut into 2-inch diamond shapes. Bake at 325 degrees for 45 minutes. Reduce the oven temperature to 300 degrees and bake for 15 minutes longer or until golden.

Combine 2 cups sugar, the water, lemon slice, orange rind and cinnamon sticks in a saucepan and bring to a boil. Boil for 20 minutes or until a light syrup forms. Remove from the heat. Stir in the honey and vanilla until blended. Remove the lemon slice, orange rind and cinnamon sticks. Cool the syrup slightly. Spoon over the baked pastry. Let stand for 4 to 24 hours before serving. To serve, separate the pieces with a sharp knife.

Serves 18

Lasagna *(Italian)*

RAGÙ ALLA BOLOGNESE
5 tablespoons extra-virgin olive oil
1/4 cup (1/2 stick) butter
1 onion, chopped
1 carrot, finely chopped
1 rib celery, finely chopped
1 garlic clove, sliced
1 pound ground beef
1 pound ground pork
4 ounces pancetta or slab of
　bacon, ground
1 (6-ounce) can tomato paste or
　homemade tomato sauce
1 cup milk
1 cup red wine
Salt and freshly ground black
　pepper to taste

Red pepper to taste
Rosemary to taste
3 or 4 bay leaves

BÉCHAMEL SAUCE
1/2 cup (1 stick) unsalted butter
1/2 cup plus 2 tablespoons
　all-purpose flour
1 quart milk, at room temperature
Pinch of freshly grated nutmeg
Sea salt and white pepper to taste

ASSEMBLY
1 (1-pound) package ready-to-bake
　lasagna pasta (Barilla preferred)
Freshly grated Parmigiano-Reggiano

To prepare the ragù alla bolognese, heat the olive oil and butter in a 6- to 8-quart heavy-bottomed saucepan over medium heat. Add the onion, carrot, celery and garlic and sweat for 10 minutes or until the vegetables are translucent and soft but not brown. Add the ground beef, ground pork and pancetta and stir to mix. Brown over high heat, stirring until crumbly. Add the tomato paste, milk and wine. Simmer over medium-low heat for at least 2 hours. Season with salt, black pepper, red pepper, rosemary and bay leaves. Cook over medium heat until of the desired consistency, stirring occasionally.

To prepare the béchamel sauce, melt the butter in a 2-quart saucepan over medium heat. Whisk in the flour. Cook for 2 minutes or until smooth, whisking constantly. Whisk in the milk gradually. Cook until the sauce is smooth and creamy, whisking constantly. Simmer for 10 minutes or until the sauce is thick enough to coat the back of a spoon. Remove from the heat. Stir in the nutmeg, sea salt and white pepper.

To assemble the lasagna, layer one-half of the béchamel sauce, the lasagna pasta, the remaining béchamel sauce, the ragù alla bolognese and the Parmigiano-Reggiano cheese in a large baking dish. Bake at 375 degrees for 30 minutes.

Serves 12

Prosciutto Wraps (Italian)

1 small leek
Salt to taste
5 each pitted green and black olives,
   cut into small pieces
6 ounces goat cheese, crumbled

3/4 cup (3 ounces) shredded Swiss
   cheese or Emmentaler cheese
1 tablespoon olive oil
Pepper and marjoram to taste
8 slices prosciutto di Parma
   or domestic prosciutto

Remove the green portion of the leek and separate the white portion into single pieces. Rinse the white portions of the leek and cook in boiling salted water in a saucepan for 2 to 3 minutes; drain and cool. Cut into 16 strips 1/3 inch wide.

Mix the olives, goat cheese and Swiss cheese in a bowl. Add the olive oil, salt, pepper and marjoram and mix well. Divide equally and place on top of the prosciutto slices. Fold the prosciutto over the filling, beginning with the small sides. Arrange 2 leek strips at a time on a flat surface to resemble a cross. Place a prosciutto parcel in the middle of each leek cross. Wrap the ends of the leek around each prosciutto parcel and arrange on a serving plate.

Makes 8

Hazelnut Biscotti (Italian)

2 3/4 cups all-purpose flour
2 1/2 teaspoons baking powder
Pinch of salt
1 1/2 cups hazelnuts, toasted and
   coarsely chopped

3 eggs
2 cups sugar
2 teaspoons vanilla extract

Mix the flour, baking powder, salt and hazelnuts in a large bowl. Whisk the eggs, sugar and vanilla in a bowl. Add to the flour mixture and stir to form a soft dough. Divide the dough into two equal portions. Shape each portion into a long roll 1 1/2 inches wide on a cookie sheet covered with baking parchment. Bake at 350 degrees for 20 minutes or until golden brown. Remove from the oven and let cool for 5 minutes. Cut each log diagonally into slices 1/2 inch thick with a sharp serrated knife, using decisive strokes to prevent crumbling. Return to the cookie sheet and bake for 10 minutes to dry. Remove from the oven to cool. Store in an airtight container for up to 2 weeks.

Makes 2 dozen

Potato Lefse (Norwegian)

2¹/4 pounds potatoes
 (about 5 large)
4 to 5 cups all-purpose flour

Softened butter
Granulated sugar or
 confectioners' sugar

Boil the unpeeled potatoes in water to cover in a saucepan until tender; drain. Cool the potatoes and peel. Press the potatoes through a potato ricer into a large bowl. Knead in enough of the flour to form a stiff dough. Divide the dough into equal-sized pieces. Roll each piece into a thin sheet and place on a hot griddle. Cook on both sides until dotted with brown, brushing the uncooked side with water before turning. Sprinkle the lefse with water and wrap in a cloth to soften. Spread the lefse with butter. Sprinkle with sugar and roll up.

Serves 12

Börek (Turkish)

1 large onion, grated
1 tablespoon olive oil
1 pound ground beef
1 teaspoon oregano

Salt and pepper to taste
12 sheets phyllo dough
1 cup (2 sticks) butter, melted

Sauté the onion in the olive oil in a skillet until translucent. Add the ground beef and cook until brown, stirring until crumbly; drain. Season with the oregano, salt and pepper.

Place 1 sheet of phyllo dough on a flat surface and brush with the melted butter, keeping the remaining phyllo dough covered with a damp cloth to prevent drying out. Cut lengthwise into 4 strips. Place a rounded teaspoon of the filling at one end of the strip. Fold the corner of the strip over the filling to meet the other side, forming a triangular fold. Continue folding the length of the strip in triangular folds to form a small stuffed triangle, making certain there are no holes. Repeat with the remaining phyllo sheets and filling. Arrange the stuffed triangles in a single layer in a lightly buttered 9×12-inch baking dish. Brush with the remaining butter. Bake at 350 degrees for 30 minutes or until light brown. Serve warm. (The börek may also be deep-fried. You may also use a cheese filling. To prepare, whisk one egg, 1 tablespoon chopped fresh parsley, one garlic clove, minced, and 1 teaspoon pepper in a bowl. Add 2 cups (8 ounces) shredded white cheese and mix well.)

Makes 4 dozen

International Flair

*T*he Junior League of Wichita Falls, Inc. is very proud of our
relationship with Sheppard Air Force Base, in particular, the Euro-NATO
Joint Jet Pilot Training program. This relationship is fostered in large part by
the League's International Friendship Committee. The ENJJPT program is
made up of instructors and student pilots from Canada, Germany, Greece,
Italy, the Netherlands, Norway, Portugal, Spain, Turkey, and the United States.
Our dear friends in this program have provided the recipes in the International
Flair section of the cookbook. We hope you find some truly different recipes
that will bring a little piece of the world to your dinner table.

Basic Substitutions

If the recipe calls for	You can substitute
Flour	
I cup sifted all-purpose flour	I cup less 2 tablespoons unsifted all-purpose flour
I cup sifted cake flour	I cup less 2 tablespoons sifted all-purpose flour
I cup sifted self-rising flour	I cup sifted all-purpose flour plus $I^{1}/2$ teaspoons baking powder and a pinch of salt
Milk/Cream	
I cup buttermilk	I cup plain yogurt, or I tablespoon lemon juice or vinegar plus enough milk to measure I cup— let stand for 5 minutes before using
I cup whipping cream or half-and-half	$7/8$ cup whole milk plus $I^{1}/2$ tablespoons butter
I cup light cream	$7/8$ cup whole milk plus 3 tablespoons butter
I cup sour cream	I cup plain yogurt
I cup sour milk	I cup plain yogurt
I cup whole milk	I cup skim or nonfat milk plus 2 tablespoons butter or margarine
Seasonings	
I teaspoon allspice	$1/2$ teaspoon cinnamon plus $1/8$ teaspoon cloves
I cup ketchup	I cup tomato sauce plus $1/2$ cup sugar plus 2 tablespoons vinegar
I teaspoon Italian spice	$1/4$ teaspoon each oregano, basil, thyme and rosemary plus dash of cayenne pepper
I teaspoon lemon juice	$1/2$ teaspoon vinegar
Sugar	
I cup confectioners' sugar	$1/2$ cup plus I tablespoon granulated sugar
I cup granulated sugar	$I^{3}/4$ cups confectioners' sugar, I cup packed light brown sugar or $3/4$ cup honey
Other	
I package active dry yeast	$1/2$ cake compressed yeast
I teaspoon baking powder	$1/4$ teaspoon cream of tartar plus $1/4$ teaspoon baking soda
I cup dry bread crumbs	$3/4$ cup cracker crumbs or I cup cornflake crumbs
I cup (2 sticks) butter	$7/8$ cup vegetable oil or I cup margarine
I tablespoon cornstarch	2 tablespoons all-purpose flour
I cup dark corn syrup	$3/4$ cup light corn syrup plus $1/4$ cup light molasses
I cup light corn syrup	I cup maple syrup
$I^{2}/3$ ounces semisweet chocolate	I ounce unsweetened chocolate plus 4 teaspoons granulated sugar
I ounce unsweetened chocolate	3 tablespoons unsweetened baking cocoa plus I tablespoon butter or margarine
I (I-ounce) square chocolate	$1/4$ cup baking cocoa plus I teaspoon shortening
I cup honey	I to $I^{1}/4$ cups sugar plus $1/4$ cup liquid, or I cup corn syrup or molasses
currants	raisins
I egg	$1/4$ cup mayonnaise

Equivalents

When the Recipe Calls for   Use

Baking

$^1/_2$ cup butter . . . . 4 ounces
2 cups butter. . . . . I pound
4 cups all-purpose flour. . . . . I pound
$4^1/_2$ to 5 cups sifted cake flour . . . . I pound
I square chocolate . . . . I ounce
I cup semisweet chocolate chips . . . . 6 ounces
4 cups marshmallows . . . . I pound
$2^1/_4$ cups packed brown sugar . . . . I pound
4 cups confectioners' sugar . . . . I pound
2 cups granulated sugar . . . . I pound

Cereal/Bread

I cup fine dry bread crumbs . . . . 4 to 5 slices
I cup soft bread crumbs . . . . 2 slices
I cup small bread cubes . . . . 2 slices
I cup fine cracker crumbs . . . . 28 saltines
I cup fine graham cracker crumbs . . . . I5 crackers
I cup vanilla wafer crumbs. . . . . 22 wafers
I cup crushed cornflakes . . . . 3 cups, uncrushed
4 cups cooked macaroni . . . . 8 ounces, uncooked
$3^1/_2$ cups cooked rice . . . . I cup, uncooked

Dairy

I cup shredded cheese . . . . 4 ounces
I cup cottage cheese. . . . . 8 ounces
I cup sour cream . . . . 8 ounces
I cup whipped cream . . . . $^1/_2$ cup heavy cream
$^2/_3$ cup evaporated milk. . . . . I small can
$I^2/_3$ cups evaporated milk . . . . I (I2-ounce) can

Fruit

4 cups sliced or chopped apples . . . . 4 medium
I cup mashed bananas . . . . 3 medium
2 cups pitted cherries . . . . 4 cups, unpitted
$2^1/_2$ cups shredded coconut . . . . 8 ounces
4 cups cranberries. . . . . I pound
I cup pitted dates . . . . I (8-ounce) package
I cup candied fruit . . . . I (8-ounce) package
3 to 4 tablespoons lemon juice plus
I tablespoon grated lemon rind . . . . I lemon
$^1/_3$ cup orange juice plus
2 teaspoons grated orange rind . . . . I orange
4 cups sliced peaches . . . . 8 medium
2 cups pitted prunes . . . . I (I2-ounce) package
3 cups raisins . . . . I (I5-ounce) package

Equivalents

When the Recipe Calls for   **Use**

Meats

4 cups chopped cooked chicken . . . . I (5-pound) chicken

3 cups chopped cooked meat . . . . I pound, cooked

2 cups cooked ground meat . . . . I pound, cooked

Nuts

I cup chopped nuts . . . . 4 ounces, shelled/I pound, unshelled

Vegetables

2 cups cooked green beans . . . . $^{1}/_{2}$ pound fresh or I (16-ounce) can

2$^{1}/_{2}$ cups lima beans or red beans . . . . I cup dried, cooked

4 cups shredded cabbage . . . . I pound

I cup grated carrot . . . . I large

8 ounces fresh mushrooms . . . . I (4-ounce) can

I cup chopped onion . . . . I large

4 cups sliced or chopped potatoes . . . . 4 medium

2 cups canned tomatoes . . . . I (16-ounce) can

Metric Equivalents

Liquid

I teaspoon = 5 milliliters

I tablespoon = 15 milliliters

I fluid ounce = 30 milliliters

I cup = 250 milliliters

I pint = 500 milliliters

Dry

I quart = I liter

I ounce = 30 grams

I pound = 450 grams

2.2 pounds = I kilogram

Measurement Equivalents

I tablespoon = 3 teaspoons

2 tablespoons = I ounce

4 tablespoons = $^{1}/_{4}$ cup

5$^{1}/_{3}$ tablespoons = $^{1}/_{3}$ cup

8 tablespoons = $^{1}/_{2}$ cup

12 tablespoons = $^{3}/_{4}$ cup

16 tablespoons = I cup

I cup = 8 ounces or $^{1}/_{2}$ pint

4 cups = I quart

4 quarts = I gallon

I (6$^{1}/_{2}$- to 8-ounce) can = I cup

I (10$^{1}/_{2}$- to 12-ounce) can = I$^{1}/_{4}$ cups

I (14- to 16-ounce) can = I$^{3}/_{4}$ cups

I (16- to 17-ounce) can = 2 cups

I (18- to 20-ounce) can = 2$^{1}/_{2}$ cups

I (29-ounce) can = 3$^{1}/_{2}$ cups

I (46- to 5I-ounce) can = 5$^{3}/_{4}$ cups

I (6$^{1}/_{2}$- to 7$^{1}/_{2}$-pound) can or
Number I0 = I2 to I3 cups

Wine Guide

Wine	Serve With
Semidry White Wines	
Bernkasteler *(Barn-kahst-ler)*	dove
Dienheimer *(Deen-heim-er)*	duck
Fendant *(Fahn-dawn)*	fish in herbed butter sauce
Frascati *(Fras-kah-tee)*	goose
Gewürztraminer	pasta
(Guh-vurts-trah-mee-ner)	quail
Johannisberg Riesling	roast turkey
(Yo-hann-is-burg Rees-ling)	salad
Kreuznach *(Kroytz-nock)*	seafood
Sylvaner Riesling	shellfish in cream sauce
(Sihl-van-uhr Rees-ling)	
Dry White Wines	
Chablis *(Sha-blee)*	chicken
Chardonnay *(Shar-doh-nay)*	cold meat
Chenin Blanc *(Shen-ihn Blahn)*	fried or grilled fish
Hermitage Blanc	ham
(Ehr-mee-tahzh Blahn)	roast young gamebirds
Meursault *(Mehr-soh)*	and waterfowl
Orvieto Secco	shellfish
(Ohr-vyay-toh Say-koh)	turkey
Piesporter Trocken	veal
(Peez-porter Trawk-uhn)	
Pinot Blanc *(Pee-noh Blahn)*	
Pinot Grigio *(Pee-noh Gree-jo)*	
Pouilly-Fuissé *(Poo-yee Fwee-say)*	
Sancerre *(Sahn-sehr)*	
Sauvignon Blanc	
(Soh-vihn-yohn Blahn)	
Soave *(So-ah-veh)*	
Verdicchio *(Vehr-deek-kyoh)*	
Vouvray *(Voo-vray)*	

Wine Guide

	Wine	Serve With

Light Red Wines	Barbera *(Bar-beh-rah)*
	Bardolino *(Bar-doh-lee-noh)*
	Beaujolais *(Boh-zhuh-lay)*
	Gamay Beaujolais
	    (Ga-may Boh-zhuh-lay)
	Lambrusco *(Lam-broos-koh)*
	Lirac *(Lee-rak)*
	Merlot del Ticino
	    (Mehr-loh dehl Tee-chee-noh)
	Moulin-à-Vent Beaujolais
	    (Moo-lan-nah-vahn Boh-zhuh-lay)
	Nuits-Saint-Georges "Villages"
	    (Nwee San Zhawrzh)
	Santa Maddalena
	    (Sahn-tah Mahd-dah-leh-nah)
	Valpolicella *(Vahl-paw-lee-chehl-lah)*
		Creole foods
		fowl with highly seasoned
		    stuffings
		grilled chicken
		lamb
		soups and stews
		veal

Hearty Red Wines	Barbaresco *(Bar-bah-ress-koh)*
	Barolo *(Bah-roh-loh)*
	Bordeaux *(Bohr-doh)*
	Burgundy *(Ber-gun-dee)*
	Cabernet Sauvignon
	    (Ka-behr-nay Soh-vihn-yohn)
	Châteauneuf-du-Pape
	    (Shah-toh-nuhf-doo-Pahp)
	Chianti Riserva
	    (Kee-ahn-tee Ree-zehr-vah)
	Côte de Beaune *(Koht duh Bohn)*
	Côte-Rotie *(Koht Roh-tee)*
	Hermitage *(Ehr-mee-tahzh)*
	Merlot *(Mehr-loh)*
	Petite Sirah *(Peh-teet Sih-rah)*
	Syrah *(See-rah)*
	Taurasi *(Tow-rah-zee)*
	Zinfandel *(Zihn-fuhn-dehl)*
		beef
		cheese and egg dishes
		duck
		goose
		hare
		highly seasoned foods
		lamb
		pastas
		pot roast
		veal
		venison

Contributors

Sincere thanks to all who submitted recipes and assisted in their preparation and testing. Without your favorite family recipes, time, financial contributions, and extensive efforts, this book would not have come to fruition.

Barbie Allen

Doris Altman

SueAnn Altman

Emily Arens

Cheri Armstrong

Susan Basham

Kerri Beaver

Melinda Berger

Jamie Berry

Rebekka Berry

Shannah Blankenship

Renee Browning

Susan Buckley

Claudette Burlison

Shawn Butler

Sheila Catron

Lee Cook

Rachelle Cooper

Sue Crosnoe

Angela Culley

Cecille Daniel

Sean Daniels, FEWMC

Joey Deal

Ruth Denman

Mary Jo Dudley

Catherine Earley

Ann Ezell

Christi Farnsworth

Pam Featherston

Keli Fields

Leah Ford

Brandy Forehand

Monta Rea Francis

Kristi Frerich

Melinda Fritsche

Karen Montgomery-Gagné

Cathy Gamble

Sara Gamble

Robin Germany

Debbie Gonzalez

Lindsay Greer

Lyndee Groce

Jennifer Haisten

Kelly Hall

Lisa Estrada-Hamby

Christy Hankins

Christie Hansard

Julie Harmon

Kristin Harris

Pam Harvey

Leslie Hawthorne

Sandy Hay

Jennifer Hinnant

Trecie Hoff

Stephanie Hollingsworth

Jennifer Hudson

Mandi Jalamo

Roxann Johnston

Stephanie Jones

Leslie Kajs

Brenda Kays

Dee King

Allison Kirkpatrick

Michaelle Kitchen

Katharina Kling, Germany

Lisa Knight

Vickie Lalani

Amy Lam

Pam Lane
Molly Lee
Rachel Liles
Leigh Anne Lilley
Merthel Lundy
Rashmi Mankodi, M.D.
Jennifer Marley
Nancy Marks
Dee Ann Martin
Wendy Matthews
Kimi McClellan
Jennifer McDonald
Anne McGaha
Tammi McGuffin
Jaclyn Meng
Kathy Mickus
Denise Moffat
Belle Morgan
Sara Neiman
Traci Neiman
Alyssa Newcomb
Vicki Ostermann
Stella Panagiotarakou, Greece
Jennifer Parker
Katie Parkey
Kathy Partridge
Donna Perkins
Paula Perkins
Janice Piper
Wendy Presson
Diane Prothro
Eva Rau, Germany
Gale Richardson
Christy Ridinger
Jeanne Rigg
Gretta Robb
Rebecca Ruddy
Carolyn Sanders

Claudette Saorski
Becky Satterfield
Leslie Schaffner
Stephanie Schelter
Becky Schroeder
Michelle Schroeder
Ina Schroth, Germany
Kristin Schuele
Claudia Schultz
Christina Scruggs
Sandy Shawver
Nancy Sherrill
Jan Slagle
Richelle Sons
Hanne Sorensen, Norway
Gloria Steimel
Theresa Strain
Susie Tanner
Joellen Tritton
Petra van Gaalen, the Netherlands
Bylinda Voigt
Carol Wagner
Deanna Watson
Laurie Welch
DeAndra West
Debbie White
Julia Whitmire
Sarah Williams
Pat Wolverton
Julie Woolsey
Tammie Wooster
Patty Young
Amy Yowell

If anyone has been inadvertently omitted from this list, please accept our deepest apologies.

Index

Bibliography

Altman Family Cookbook *(not copyrighted)*

Web Site Resources:
www.foodreference.com
www.pazsaz.com
www.quotegarden.com

The Junior League of Wichita Falls, Inc.
Attention: Cookbook
2302 Midwestern Parkway
Wichita Falls, Texas 76308-2328
940-692-9797
www.jlwf.org

Name

Street Address

City   State   Zip

Telephone   E-mail

YOUR ORDER	QTY	TOTAL
Now Serving at $26.95 per book		$
Texas residents add 8.25% sales tax		$
Postage and handling at $4.50 per book		$
TOTAL		$

Method of Payment:* [ ] MasterCard   [ ] VISA

                        [ ] Check enclosed payable to The Junior League of Wichita Falls, Inc.

Account Number   Expiration Date

Cardholder Name

Signature

*Additional $2.00 fee when purchasing with credit card.

Photocopies accepted.